DATE DUE

Feb 22'64		

F

"A professor can never better distinguish himself in his work than by encouraging a clever pupil, for the true discoverers are among them, as comets amongst the stars."

CAROLUS LINNAEUS
1707–1778

FOUNDATIONS

OF MODERN

GENERAL

CHEMISTRY

SERIES

Man-Made

Transuranium

Elements

Glenn T. Seaborg

PRENTICE-HALL, INC., Englewood Cliffs, N. J.

To: Peter, Lynne, David, Stephen, John Eric, and Dianne

With the hope that they may read this book now or later.

546.43
Sebm

45920
Oct. 1963

FOUNDATIONS OF MODERN GENERAL CHEMISTRY SERIES

Robert W. Parry and Henry Taube, Editors

This monograph is designed as an extension of CHEM Study materials

Preface

The discovery and study of the trans-uranium elements is one of the latest and most vital extensions in chemistry. With these discoveries, man has been able to create new elements. Exemplary of these new elements is plutonium, the second transuranium element discovered. It was the first synthetic element seen by man and the first example of large-scale production of an element by transmutation. Plutonium was discovered and the methods for its manufacture were worked out during the last war. Its discovery was announced to the world when a plutonium bomb was dropped on Nagasaki. Plutonium has begun to play an important role in the peaceful applications of nuclear energy to the production of electrical power. Plutonium and other transuranium isotopes also promise to be useful sources of concentrated isotopic power for use in space, as well as for application on earth, by virtue of the energy released in their radioactive decay.

In writing this book, I have had in mind readers equipped with an understanding of the basic principles of physics and chemistry, although Part I can be read with profit by those with less preparation than this. It is hoped that this treatment of important aspects of post-World War II chemistry

v

will encourage further exploration by the reader. A list of references is therefore supplied at the close of the book.

The chapters which follow are grouped into two parts. The first deals with a chronological and comprehensive survey of each of the eleven transuranium elements discovered before 1963. It also discusses the position of these elements in the Periodic Table, the experimental methods of chemical investigation used in their discovery and study, the prospects for future transuranium elements, and, finally, treats the present and future applications of the transuranium elements.

Part II offers a more detailed account of the chemical and physical parameters of the actinide elements (electronic structure, chemical and physical properties, and nuclear properties) and investigates the sources of these elements. Although the transuranium elements begin with neptunium, these elements, through lawrencium, belong to the actinide (actinium-like) series, with element number 89, actinium, as the prototype. The section is intended to serve as a source of reference material for the general student and provides further material for the more advanced student.

This book has been written for use with the Chemical Education Material Study—i.e., CHEM Study—of which the author serves as Chairman; CHEM Study is a high school Course Content Improvement Study supported by the National Science Foundation and centered at the University of California, Berkeley, and Harvey Mudd College, Claremont, California, In this connection, it supplements Chapter 23 of the CHEM Study textbook *Chemistry—An Experimental Science*. The book has been written, however, with the view that it might find, in addition, more general use by those interested for any reason in the transuranium elements.

The author wishes to thank a number of people who read the manuscript in preliminary form. The helpful suggestions of B. B. Cunningham, E. K. Hyde, and J. J. Katz, were based on the reading of the entire manuscript. I. Perlman and S. G. Thompson helped in the preparation of Chapter 10. Miss Eileen Carson, D. C. Clark, C. Heslep, and D. R. Miller also made welcome suggestions for improvement. Special thanks are due to A. R. Fritsch for his help in all phases of the writing project and to Miss Gloria Lettre for her role in the preparation of the manuscript.

Glenn T. Seaborg

Chairman, U. S. Atomic Energy Commission
Washington, D. C.

Contents

PART ONE

1   *Introduction,*   1

2   *Discovery
of the
Transuranium Elements,*   6

3   *Position
in the Periodic Table,*   37

4   *Experimental Chemical
Methods of Investigation,*   42

5   *Future
Transuranium Elements,*   52

6   *Application
of the
Transuranium Elements,*   58

vii

P A R T   T W O

7   *Source
of the Actinide Elements,*   68

8   *Electronic Structure
of the Actinide Elements,*   79

9   *Chemical
and Physical Properties
of the Actinide Elements,*   83

10   *Nuclear Properties
of the Actinide Elements,*   95

Postscript,   109

Suggested Further Readings, 109

Appendix,   110

Index,   118

1

Introduction

The study of the "transuranium elements"—the chemical elements with atomic numbers greater than that of the heaviest naturally-occurring element, uranium—is an exciting branch of science which started as recently as World War II and which undoubtedly will undergo great expansion in the future. The transuranium elements represent the realization of the alchemists' dream of transmutation. They are, for all practical purposes, "synthetic" in origin—that is, they must be produced by transmutation, if we start in the first instance with naturally-occurring uranium. But before examining these elements in any detail, it might perhaps be well to start this study with the explanation of a few basic terms and principles.

The nomenclature of the nucleus of the atom is of fundamental importance. The *atomic number* of an element is determined by the number of *protons* (fundamental particles carrying one unit of positive charge with a mass about 1850 times that of the electron) in the nucleus of the atom. *Isotopes* of an element are essentially chemically identical forms of *nuclides* (atomic species), each containing the same number of protons. Isotopes, however, differ in the number of *neutrons* (fundamental particles, electrically-neutral, with about the same atomic mass as protons). Thus, isotopes differ in *mass number,* the integral sum of *nucleons* (the collective name for protons and neutrons) in the nucleus. The nuclear *strange particles—* mesons, hyperons, etc.—created and studied in high-energy nuclear physics, need not be considered here. *Isobars* are nuclides with the same mass number, but differing in atomic number. The *atomic mass* is the exact weight of the atom (nucleus plus electrons) relative to that of the nuclide C^{12}, which has been assigned an atomic mass equal to 12. Thus, as illustrations, among the three nuclides Np^{239}, Pu^{238}, and Pu^{239}, we have: (a) the two isotopes of plutonium, Pu^{238} and Pu^{239}; (b) the isobars Np^{239} and Pu^{239}; (c) the mass numbers 239, 238, and 239, respectively; and (d) the atomic masses 239.05061, 238.04717, and 239.04982, respectively.

In "synthesizing" a new element, it is necessary to begin with an element present in the natural world or available from a previous synthesis. Then, by a suitable process of nuclear transmutation, atoms of the starting element are converted into the atoms of the desired new element. Since the number of protons existing in the atomic nucleus determines what the element is, the "synthesis" of a new element involves an increase in the number of protons in the nucleus of the starting material.

New elements have been "synthesized" in different ways. They have been produced in nuclear reactors, as products of the explosion of nuclear devices, and by the use of particle accelerators (popularly called "atom smashers"). In both a nuclear reactor or a nuclear explosion, the atomic nucleus of the starting element is subjected to bombardment with neutrons. Because neutrons are electrically neutral, they have little difficulty in entering the nucleus, where they are absorbed and bound to other neutrons and to protons by strong, short-range, nuclear forces. This, in itself, does not create a new element, because the capture of a neutron does not affect the number of protons in the nucleus. Rather, a new isotope of the starting element is created.

A second process must therefore occur before the nucleus of the new isotope of the starting element is converted into a nucleus of a new element. This conversion of one isobar to a neighboring isobar is a radioactive change called *beta decay.* This radioactive change occurs because the forces binding protons and neutrons together in the nucleus are strongest when the ratio of protons and neutrons is close to a certain favored value. When this ratio is disturbed by the addition of a neutron, the resulting nucleus may seek to achieve greater stability by converting a neutron into a proton. In order to conserve the electric charge, a negative beta particle (*electron*) is created during this process and it is ejected from the nucleus with great kinetic energy. This process of conversion of a neutron into a proton is a spontaneous process which may occur in a few seconds or a few minutes, or it may take years. This is one type of spontaneous nuclear transmutation to which is given the general name, *radioactivity.* Although negative beta decay is described in this case, another nucleus deficient in neutrons can convert a proton into a neutron, through the emission of a positive beta particle (*positron*) or by the capture of an *orbital electron,* thus reducing its atomic number by one unit. After the nucleus has emitted a negative or positive beta particle, the balance of nuclear charge and that of the total orbital (extra nuclear) electrons is disturbed; the atom is then in an ionized state until orbital electrons are acquired from or lost to the environment.

The third method of synthesizing an element is based on the bombardment of the starting element by the nuclei of light elements. Protons (the nuclei of the element hydrogen), deuterons (the nuclei of a heavy isotope of hydrogen), or the nuclei of helium, carbon, nitrogen, oxygen, or other elements, can be used as projectiles. The protons present in both the target element and in the bombarding nuclei have a positive electrical charge; therefore, they experience strong repulsion when they approach each other. Nuclei must actually touch each other if any transmutation is to occur, and since nuclear diameters are very small, the positive charges must be brought very close to each other. This requires that the kinetic energy of the bombarding particle be very large. High-voltage machinery known as *particle accelerators* (for example, cyclotrons and linear accelerators) are devices for achieving the enormous energies required to cause nuclear reactions, i.e., to get nuclei of one kind of atom to penetrate the nuclei of other atoms.

Once the bombarding nucleus penetrates the target nucleus, the short-range nuclear forces bind the two nuclei together into a *compound nucleus*. This creates the nucleus of a new element, since there are now more protons than there were in the original nucleus. The newly-created, intermediate compound nucleus possesses a certain amount of *excitation energy* (energy in excess of that of the lowest energy state of the nucleus) which must be dissipated before the nucleus can stabilize.

In the heaviest elements like the transuranium elements, in the cases where fission does not occur, this extra energy is usually dissipated by the emission of *gamma rays* (high-energy electromagnetic radiation) and the "boiling off" of neutrons from the excited nucleus. (Other nuclear reactions, of course, can also occur.) The nucleus of the new element is radioactive, and it will strive to achieve greater stability by changing its internal constitution through radioactive decay (*beta-* or *alpha-particle decay,* or *spontaneous fission*) which is further described in Chapter 10. The radioactive decay of each individual nuclear species proceeds at a rate which is characteristic of that species. The decay of such a species is described in terms of a *half-life* ($T_{1/2}$), which is the period of time required for one-half of its atoms to disintegrate.

When the nuclear transformation is completed, a new element still has not been discovered. Certain tests must be performed to prove that the hypothetical new element does, in fact, have an atomic number different from those of all known elements. This may be done by showing that the new element has unique chemical properties. This is not an easy task, however, because of the small number of atoms available for study and because of the short time usually available to study the new element before it undergoes radioactive decay. In fact, for the last two transuranium elements produced (elements 102 and 103), it has not been possible so far to perform chemical tests, and knowledge of their discovery rests on physical analyses and other related evidence.

It is important to realize that in these nuclear reactions (particularly under the experimental conditions used in the first synthesis) very few of the atoms of the target element are converted into atoms of the new element. When all of these atoms are collected in one spot, it is still quite impossible to see them, to weigh them, or to perform any of the normal chemical tests which one would make on a *macroscopic* (visible or weighable) quantity of material. Hence, the chemical properties of the new elements must be studied by special techniques which are known by the general name of *tracer chemistry* or *radiochemistry*. A brief description of this technique is included in Chapter 4, as well as in Chapter 2 in the section on "Neptunium."

It is usually some time after the discovery of the new element that larger, visible amounts of the material are first produced and first isolated from all the other elements listed in the Periodic Table. These visible amounts of a new element can then be weighed and examined in a pure form and the macroscopic properties of the element and its compounds studied.

The key to the discovery of the transuranium elements has been their position in the Periodic Table. Prior to the discovery of the transuranium elements, the relationship of the naturally-occurring elements—thorium (atomic number 90), protactinium (number 91), and uranium (number 92)—in the Periodic Table was not clearly understood. Recognition of the fact that the transuranium elements represented a whole new family of *actinide* ("like actinium"—atomic number 89) elements analogous to the *lanthanide* (rare earth) series of elements (atomic numbers 58 through 71), permitted the discoverers to predict the chemical properties of the unknown transuranium elements. Once these properties were predicted, it was possible to discover the new elements by chemically separating them from all the other elements in the Periodic Table.

By 1963, eleven transuranium elements had been created (Table 1).

Table 1 THE ATOMIC NUMBERS, NAMES, AND SYMBOLS OF THE TRANSURANIUM ELEMENTS

Atomic Number	Name	Symbol
93	Neptunium	Np
94	Plutonium	Pu
95	Americium	Am
96	Curium	Cm
97	Berkelium	Bk
98	Californium	Cf
99	Einsteinium	Es
100	Fermium	Fm
101	Mendelevium	Md
102	(Name to be chosen) *	
103	Lawrencium	Lw

* See pages 31–33.

It may still prove to be possible to separate and identify a half-dozen or so more of the transuranium elements; but barring unknown experimental developments or the discovery of unknown regions of stability in these heavier elements, the end will probably come somewhere in the region of element 110. The elements up to and including einsteinium have isotopes sufficiently long-lived to be isolated and studied with macroscopic quantities, but this does not seem to be true for elements beyond einsteinium (except for extremely unusual and limited experiments). Unfortunately, at some atomic number below 110, difficult at present to estimate, the longest-lived isotopes that can be made apparently will not exist long enough for the performance of conventional types of tracer chemical experiments.

Problems inherent in the study of these elements, such as those of handling quantities of material so small as to be unweighable (in some cases as small as only an atom or two), of handling weighable quantities as small as one-billionth of an ounce, of working in safety with highly-radioactive materials, and of preparing and identifying elements of ever-increasing atomic number, have been or are being solved. Neptunium is available in the form of an isotope of sufficiently long half-life to be safe to handle with moderate precautions in ordinary laboratories. Plutonium and curium also have long-lived isotopes that eventually should make these elements available for broader investigation throughout the world.

Plutonium has most unusual chemical and metallurgical properties. For example, it has four oxidation states that may exist in aqueous solution in equilibrium with each other at appreciable concentrations. Plutonium metal has six stable forms between room tempearture and its melting point; some of these forms have properties unknown in any other metal. The alpha-radioactivity of several plutonium isotopes and their behavior in the body make plutonium one of the most toxic substances known. It is therefore a favorable commentary on the resources of modern chemistry that this element has been so thoroughly studied with relatively little hazard to the investigators (see Chapter 4).

The relationship of the transuranium elements to each other, and to the other elements of the Periodic Table, is now within our understanding. As might be expected, an advance in science as fundamental as a 12 per cent increase in the number of chemical elements has contributed much to our fund of basic scientific knowledge, especially in the fields of chemistry and physics. For example, since the transuranium elements have a rich and varied chemical behavior, exemplified by the formation of unusual compounds and by the extraordinary complexity of their ions in solution, investigation of these new transuranium elements has made major contributions to inorganic chemistry and has helped to stimulate the recent renaissance in that field. Similarly, study of the radioactive and fission properties of the approximately 100-known transuranium nuclear species has added significantly to our understanding of nuclear structure.

2

Discovery

of the Transuranium

Elements

The efforts of men to change one element to another, or to create new elements, date back to the time of the alchemists and even earlier. But the first scientific attempts to prepare elements beyond uranium and to explore the transuranium area were by Enrico Fermi, Emilio Segrè, and co-workers in Rome in 1934, shortly after the existence of the neutron was discovered.

This group of investigators bombarded uranium with slow neutrons and found a number of radioactive products. In the years immediately following, many more such radioactive species were observed. Chemical investigations (see first section of Chapter 3), showed, however, that these species were isotopes of known elements formed by the splitting or *nuclear fission* of uranium atoms into two approximately equal parts. Dozens of pairs of radioactive (beta-particle emitting) fission products are formed in reactions of a type exemplified by the following:

$$_{92}U^{235} + {_0}n^1 \longrightarrow {_{56}}Ba^{140} +$$

$$_{36}Kr^{93} + 3{_0}n^1 + energy$$

This discovery of nuclear fission by O. Hahn and F.S. Strassmann, in December of 1938, which led to the "atomic age," was thus a by-product of man's quest for the transuranium elements.

Curiously enough, the discovery of the first transuranium element, neptunium, was in turn a by-product of studies conducted of the fission process by E.M. McMillan in 1940. Following the discovery and study of the first new elements, the chemical behavior of the transuranium elements and their position in the Periodic Table became clarified, and the discovery of the remaining elements followed in a logical manner.

The discovery of each of the transuranium elements is described in detail and in chronological order in the following sections. It is well to emphasize, again, that there is a distinction between the *discovery* of an element —meaning the first nuclear and chemical proof of the existence of atoms of a new element—and the first *isolation* of an element, i.e., the first isolation of a weighable amount in pure form.

Neptunium

E.M. McMillan, working at the University of California at Berkeley in the spring of 1940, was trying to measure the energies of the two main recoiling fragments from the neutron-induced fission of uranium. He placed a thin layer of uranium oxide on one piece of paper, and next to this he stacked very thin paper sheets to stop and collect the fission fragments from uranium. The paper he used was ordinary cigarette paper, the kind used by people who roll their own cigarettes. In the course of his studies, he found that there was another radioactive product of the reaction—one that did not recoil sufficiently to escape from the thin layer of uranium undergoing fission, as do the fission products. He suspected that this was a product formed by neutron capture in the abundant, relatively non-fissionable isotope of uranium, uranium-238. McMillan—and P.H. Abelson, who joined him in this research—were able to show, on the basis of their chemical work, that this product is an isotope of element 93, neptunium-239, formed by neutron capture and beta decay, with a half-life of 23.5 minutes:

$$_{92}U^{238} + {}_0n^1 \longrightarrow {}_{92}U^{239} + \gamma$$

$$_{92}U^{239} \xrightarrow[T_{1/2} = 23.5 \text{ m}]{\beta^-} {}_{93}Np^{239} \ (T_{1/2} = 2.35 \text{ d})$$

These reactions can also be written in a sort of shorthand notation, as $U^{238} (n, \gamma) U^{239}$, depicting the capture of the neutron followed by de-excitation by the emission of gamma rays, and as $U^{239} \beta^-$ decay. This illustrates the system used in the Appendix, where the nuclear reactions for producing each of the transuranium nuclides are summarized.

The 60-inch cyclotron of the Crocker Radiation Laboratory, on the Berkeley campus of the University of California, was used to furnish the neutrons for these bombardments of uranium. This cyclotron was used in the discovery of six of the transuranium elements (neptunium, plutonium, curium, berkelium, californium, and mendelevium). It has since been moved to the Davis campus of the University to be used, after renovation and modernization, for further research in nuclear chemistry and physics.

In 1940 it was not apparent what the electron arrangement of neptunium would be; consequently, the chemical properties of the new element could not be predicted. Uranium was known to have some similarity to tungsten, and at that time it was thought that element 93 might resemble rhenium, the element beyond tungsten in the Periodic Table. There was the possibility, however, that neptunium might be a member of some new type of closely-related, consecutive series of elements (transition series) among the heavy elements. The experimental investigation of neptunium by McMillan and Abelson showed that it resembles uranium, not rhenium, in its chemical properties. This was the first definite evidence that an inner electron shell (the so-called 5f shell which is described in Chapter 8) is filled in the transuranium region of elements. The consequence of such filling, as in the case of the rare-earth elements, is that the outer electrons, which largely determine chemical behavior, remain much the same; this leads to a series of chemically similar elements.

The early investigation of neptunium, as is the case with all of the transuranium elements, was not done with weighable quantities of material, but was carried out by the tracer technique. In this procedure, the course of the element is followed or "traced" through various chemical separations by observing the radioactive decay of the element (see Chapter 4). Since the decay of a single atom of the element can be detected by measurement of its radiation with a suitable counter, it is easy to tell in which fraction (precipitate or solution, for example) the element is contained, even though only a few atoms are present. In spite of the minute quantities involved, these methods can be used to deduce, in an approximate way, much information about the chemical properties of an element—for example, the solubility of its compounds, its oxidation-reduction potentials, and its formation of complex ions. Thus, by use of tracer techniques during the initial studies of neptunium, it was possible to show that at least two different oxidation states exist (see the discussion of plutonium).

The first isolation of a weighable amount of neptunium in the form of the long-lived isotope, neptunium-237, had to wait until October, 1944, when L.B. Magnusson and T.J. LaChappelle were able to isolate the material at the wartime Metallurgical Laboratory of the University of Chicago. The neptunium was produced in a nuclear reactor as a by-product of the beta decay of uranium-237 formed by a nuclear reaction on uranium-238. The nuclear reactions involved are:

$$_{92}U^{238} + {}_0n^1 \longrightarrow {}_{92}U^{237} + 2{}_0n^1$$

$$_{92}U^{237} \xrightarrow[T_{1/2} = 6.8 \text{ d}]{\beta^-} {}_{93}Np^{237} \ (T_{1/2} = 2.20 \times 10^6 \text{ y})$$

The shorthand notation for the first reaction, above, is U^{238} (n, 2n) U^{237}.

FIGURE 1. *First neptunium compound isolated (magnified approximately sixteen - and - one - half times). The neptunium present as the oxide, appears at the bottom (left end) of the horizontal capillary tube. The sample was isolated in 1944 and weighed about 10 micrograms. Below the sample, for purposes of comparison, is a millimeter scale, and above it is a dime (U.S. ten cent piece) for purposes of comparison.*

A photograph of this first preparation of a macroscopic amount of a pure neptunium compound is shown in Figure 1. After this isolation, the properties of neptunium could be studied using weighable, i.e., macroscopic, quantities, although it was necessary to use the methods of microchemistry and ultramicrochemistry to examine the small amounts available. (See the discussion of plutonium.)

Neptunium was named after the planet Neptune because it is beyond uranium, just as the planet Neptune is beyond Uranus for which uranium was named.

Plutonium

Plutonium was the second transuranium element to be discovered. By bombarding uranium with deuterons, the heavy isotope of hydrogen, in the 60-inch cyclotron at Berkeley, E.M. McMillan, J.W. Kennedy, A.C. Wahl, and the author, in late 1940, succeeded in preparing a new isotope of neptunium-238, which decayed to plutonium-238:

$$_{92}U^{238} + {}_1H^2 \longrightarrow {}_{93}Np^{238} + 2\,{}_0n^1$$

$$_{93}Np^{238} \xrightarrow[T_{1/2} = 2.10 \text{ d}]{\beta^-} {}_{94}Pu^{238} \ (T_{1/2} = 86.4 \text{ y})$$

In this case, the shorthand notation is U^{238} (d, 2n) Np^{238}.

The first bombardment of uranium oxide with 16-Mev deuterons was performed on December 14, 1940. *Alpha radioactivity* (the process of radioactive decay whereby an alpha particle, the nucleus of a helium atom $_2He^4$, is emitted and a new daughter atom, with a decrease of 2 in the atomic number and approximately 4 in atomic mass, is formed) was found to grow into the chemically-separated element 93 fraction during the following weeks. This alpha activity was chemically separated from the neighboring elements, especially elements 90 to 93 inclusive, in experiments performed during the next two months. These experiments, which constituted the positive identification of element 94, showed that this element has at least two oxidation states, distinguishable by their tracer precipitation chemistry, and that stronger oxidizing agents are required to oxidize element 94 to the upper state than is the case for element 93, neptunium. The first successful oxidation of element 94, which probably represents the key step in its discovery, was effected by the use of peroxydisulfate ion and silver ion catalyst during the night of February 23, 1941.

The chemical properties of elements 93 and 94 were studied by the tracer method at the University of California for the next year-and-a-half. These first two transuranium elements were referred to simply as "element 93" and "element 94," or by code names, until the spring of 1942, at which time the first detailed reports on this work were written. The early work, even in those days, was carried on under a self-imposed cover of secrecy, in view of the potential military application of element 94. Throughout 1941, element 94 was referred to by the code name of "copper," which was satisfactory until it was necessary to introduce the element copper into some of the experiments. This posed the problem of distinguishing between the two. For a while, plutonium was referred to as "copper" and the real copper as "honest-to-God copper."

This offered more and more difficulties as time went on, and element 94 was finally christened "plutonium" in March of 1942. Plutonium was named after the planet Pluto, following the pattern used in naming neptunium. Pluto is the second and last known planet beyond Uranus.

Because of its ability to undergo fission and thereby serve as a source of nuclear energy similar to uranium-235, the plutonium isotope with the mass number 239 is the one of major importance. The search for this isotope, as a decay product of neptunium-239, was being conducted by J.W. Kennedy, E. Segrè, A.C. Wahl, and the author, simultaneously with experiments leading to the discovery of plutonium. The isotope plutonium-239 was identified and its possibilities as a nuclear energy source were established during the spring of 1941. Plutonium-239 was produced by the decay of neptunium-239, which in turn was produced from uranium-238 by neutrons from the 60-inch cyclotron in the Crocker Laboratory:

$$_{92}U^{238} + _0n^1 \longrightarrow _{92}U^{239} + \gamma$$

$$_{92}U^{239} \xrightarrow[\text{T}_{1/2} = 23.5 \text{ m}]{\beta^-} {}_{93}Np^{239} \xrightarrow[\text{T}_{1/2} = 2.35 \text{ d}]{\beta^-} {}_{94}Pu^{239} \; (\text{T}_{1/2} = 24{,}360 \text{ y})$$

A sample of uranyl nitrate weighing 1.2 kilograms was distributed in a large paraffin block (neutron-slowing material) placed directly behind the beryllium target of the 60-inch cyclotron and was bombarded for two days with neutrons produced by the impact of the full deuteron beam on beryllium. The irradiated uranyl nitrate was placed in a continuously-operating glass extraction apparatus, and the uranyl nitrate was extracted into diethyl ether. Neptunium-239 was isolated by use of the oxidation-reduction principle (described later in this section) with lanthanum and cerium fluoride carrier and was reprecipitated six times in order to remove all uranium impurity. Measurement of the radiation from the neptunium-239 made it possible to calculate that 0.5 microgram was present to yield plutonium-239 upon decay. The resulting alpha activity corresponded to a half-life of 30,000 years for the daughter plutonium-239, in demonstrable agreement with the present best value for the half-life of 24,360 years.

The group first demonstrated, on March 28, 1941, with the sample containing 0.5 microgram of plutonium-239, that this isotope undergoes slow neutron-induced fission with a probability of reaction (*cross section*) even larger than that of uranium-235. The sample was placed near the screened window of an ionization chamber that could detect the fissions of plutonium-239. Neutrons were then produced near the sample by bombarding a beryllium target with deuterons in the 37-inch cyclotron of Berkeley's "Old Radiation Laboratory" (the name applied to the original wooden building, since torn down to make way for modern buildings). Paraffin around the sample slowed the neutrons down so they would be captured more readily by the plutonium. This experiment gave a small but detectable fission rate when a six microampere beam of deuterons was used. To increase the accuracy of the measurement of the fission cross section, this sample, which had about five milligrams of rare-earth carrier materials, was subjected to an oxidation-reduction chemical procedure that reduced the amount of carrier to a few tenths of a milligram. A fission cross section for plutonium-239, some 50 per cent greater than that for uranium-235, was found, agreeing remarkably with the accurate values that were determined later.

Once it was realized that plutonium, as plutonium-239, might be used to make a nuclear weapon and that it might be created in quantity in a nuclear chain reactor followed by separation from uranium and the highly radioactive fission products (see Chapter 6), it became imperative to carry out chemical investigations of plutonium to develop large-scale chemical separations procedures. Once again, it was necessary to use code names to maintain secrecy, and a general numbering system—using the last numerals of the atomic number and mass number—was evolved for use in referring to any of a number of nuclides. Thus, in the case of plutonium-239, i.e., 94-239, the code number was "49"; those who worked on this project now refer to themselves as "forty-niners."

These investigations required that some of the work be done with weighable quantities, even though only microgram quantities could be produced using the cyclotron sources of neutrons available at that time. In August, 1942, B.B. Cunningham and L.B. Werner, working at the wartime Metallurgical Laboratory at the University of Chicago, succeeded in isolating about a microgram of plutonium-239 which had been prepared by cyclotron irradiations. Thus, plutonium was the first man-made element to be obtained in visible quantity. The first weighing of this man-made element, using a larger sample, was made by these investigators on September 10, 1942. A photograph of this material is shown in Figure 2.

A background of manipulative techniques for this *ultramicrochemical* work was provided by the pioneer investigations of P.L. Kirk and A.A. Benedetti-Pichler. If extremely small volumes are used, even microgram quantities of material can give relatively high concentrations in solution; and with the development of balances of the required sensitivity, microgram amounts were also sufficient for gravimetric analysis. Liquid volumes in the range of 10^{-1} cc to 10^{-5} cc were measured with an error of less than one per cent by means of finely-calibrated capillary tubing. The movement of liquid was controlled by air pressure. Smaller pipettes were constructed which filled by capillary action. Chemical glassware, such as test tubes and beakers, was constructed from capillary tubing having an internal diameter of 0.1 to 1 mm and was handled with micromanipulators. The weights of solid reagents and precipitates handled in ultramicrochemical work are usually in the range of 0.1 to 100 micrograms. Solids are usually separated from liquids by centrifuging rather than by filtration. The chemical work usually is done on the mechanical stage of a microscope, as shown in Figure 3, where the essential apparatus is within view. Figures 4 and 5 show schematic drawings of the experimental arrangements used in the first preparation of pure plutonium metal and pure plutonium trichloride.

FIGURE 2. *First plutonium compound to be weighed, September 10, 1942. (Magnified approximately fifty times.) The plutonium, present as the oxide, appears as a crusty deposit, indicated by the arrow, near the end of a platinum weighing boat which is held by forceps. The weight of the plutonium oxide was 2.77 milligrams.*

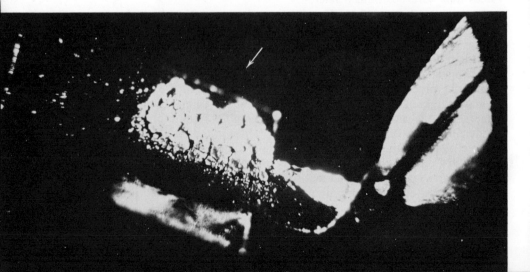

Plutonium is now produced in much larger quantities than any other synthetic element. The large wartime chemical separation plant at Hanford, Washington, was constructed on the basis of investigations performed on the ultramicrochemical scale of investigation. The scale-up between ultra-microchemical experiments and the final Hanford plant corresponds to a factor of about 1,000,000,000, surely a scale-up of unique proportions.

The ultramicrochemical work on the Hanford chemical separation process was preceded by tracer work. As a result of tracer investigations during 1941 and early 1942 at the University of California, a great deal was learned about the chemical properties of plutonium. It was established that it had at least two oxidation states, the higher of which was not "carried" by lanthanum fluoride or cerium fluoride, while the lower state was quan-titatively coprecipitated with these compounds.

FIGURE 3. *Experimental arrangement for the study of precipitation reactions on the microgram scale.*

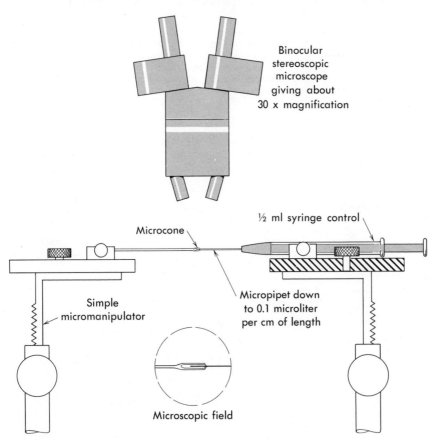

The principle of the oxidation-reduction cycle was conceived and applied to the separation processes that were to become so useful later. This principle, as applied to precipitation processes, involved the use of a carrier substance which would retain plutonium in one of its oxidation states but not in another. In practice, the Hanford chemical separation process, first worked out on the tracer scale at the Chicago wartime Metallurgical Laboratory, used a precipitate of bismuth phosphate to "carry" the plutonium in the IV oxidation state. The fission products, some of which were also "carried" and therefore accompanied the plutonium, were removed by dissolving the bismuth phosphate, oxidizing the plutonium to the VI oxidation state, and then reprecipitating the bismuth phosphate. Plutonium in the higher oxidation state was not carried by a bismuth phosphate precipitate, while the fission products behaved as previously and again were carried by the bismuth phosphate. The plutonium was then reduced to the IV oxidation state and the *decontamination* cycle repeated in order to effect still further separation.

Even today, chemical investigations of plutonium and of other transuranium elements are frequently carried out on a scale of a milligram or

FIGURE 4. *Apparatus used in the first preparation of plutonium metal, November, 1943. Treating 35 micrograms of plutonium tetrafloride with volatilized barium metal in a thoria crucible at 1400°C., this first preparation produced metallic plutonium as silvery globules weighing about 3 micrograms each.*

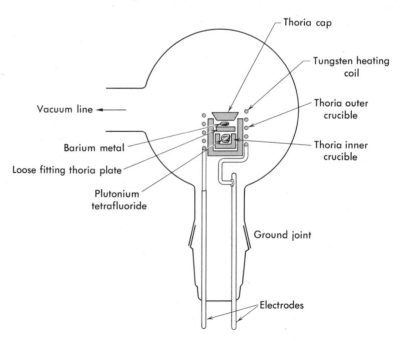

less by choice, rather than from any limitation of supply. Plutonium-239 is exceedingly toxic because of its high alpha-radioactivity, amounting to about 140,000,000 alpha-disintegrations per minute per milligram, and because it tends to be retained by the body; special equipment and precautions are necessary when working with it (described in Chapter 4).

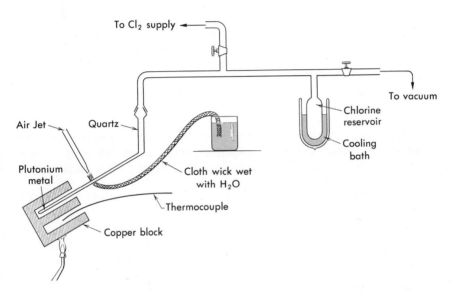

FIGURE 5. *Apparatus used in the first preparation of PuCl₃, February, 1944. The compound was prepared by treating a 50 microgram piece of plutonium metal with chlorine gas. After placing the plutonium in the capillary tube, the system was evacuated. Chlorine gas was added, and a small amount condensed in a reservoir as shown. The system was closed and remained filled with chlorine at a pressure of about 60 mm Hg. The copper block was heated to 45°C, and the reaction product was formed in the top of the capillary tube. The section of the capillary containing the product was sealed off and the compound formed was identified by X-ray diffraction.*

Americium and Curium

At the wartime Metallurgical Laboratory, after the completion of the most essential part of the chemical investigations involved in the production of plutonium, attention was turned to the synthesis and identification of the next transuranium elements. A. Ghiorso, R.A. James, L.O. Morgan, and the author, were collaborators in this endeavor.

There followed a period during which the attempts to synthesize and identify elements 95 and 96 bore no fruit. The unsuccessful experiments were based on the premise that these elements should be much like plutonium, by the fact that it should be possible readily to oxidize them to the VI oxidation state and to utilize this state in the chemical isolation procedures. It was not until the middle of the summer of 1944, when it was first recognized that these elements were part of an actinide transition series (discussed further in the next chapter), that any advance was made. Progress then came quickly.

Once it was realized that these elements could be oxidized above the III state only with difficulty, the use of a proper chemical procedure led quickly to the identification of an isotope of a transplutonium element. Thus, the isotope now known to be curium-242 (half-life 162.5 d) was produced in the summer of 1944 by the bombardment of plutonium-239 with 32-Mev helium ions:

$$_{94}Pu^{239} + {}_2He^4 \longrightarrow {}_{96}Cm^{242}\ (T_{1/2} = 162.5\ d) + {}_0n^1$$

The shorthand notation is $Pu^{239}\ (\alpha, n)\ Cm^{242}$. The bombardment took place in the Berkeley 60-inch cyclotron, after which the material was shipped to the Metallurgical Laboratory at Chicago for chemical separation and identification.

The identification of element 95 followed, by late 1944 and early 1945, as a result of the bombardment of plutonium-239 with neutrons in a reactor; the production reactions being:

$$_{94}Pu^{239} + {}_0n^1 \longrightarrow {}_{94}Pu^{240}\ (T_{1/2} = 6580\ y) + \gamma$$

$$_{94}Pu^{240} + {}_0n^1 \longrightarrow {}_{94}Pu^{241} + \gamma$$

$$_{94}Pu^{241} \xrightarrow[\;T_{1/2} = 13.2\ y\;]{\beta^-} {}_{95}Am^{241}\ (T_{1/2} = 458\ y)$$

Some comments should be made, at this point, concerning the similarity of these two elements to the rare-earth elements. Our hypothesis that elements 95 and 96 should have a stable III oxidation state and greatly resemble the rare-earth elements in their chemical properties proved to be true. In fact, the near identity of their properties greatly hindered our efforts. The better part of a year was spent in trying, without success, to separate chemically the two elements from each other and from the fission product and carrier rare-earth elements. Although we were confident, on the basis of their chemical and radioactive properties and the methods of production, that isotopes of elements 95 and 96 had been produced, the complete chemical proof still was undemonstrated. The elements remained unnamed during this period of futile attempt at separation (although one of the group referred to them as "pandemonium" and "delirium" in recognition of our difficulties). The key to their chemical separation, which occurred later at Berkeley, and the technique which made feasible the separation and identification of the subsequent transuranium elements was the ion-exchange technique, which is described in Chapter 4.

The present names of these new elements were proposed on the basis of their chemical properties. The name "americium" was suggested for element 95, after the Americas, by analogy with the naming of its rare-earth counterpart or homologue, europium, after Europe; and the name "curium" was suggested for element 96, after Pierre and Marie Curie, by analogy with the naming of its homologue, gadolinium, after the Finnish rare-earth chemist, J. Gadolin.

By chance, the discovery of these elements was revealed informally on a nationally-broadcast radio program, the Quiz Kids, on which the author appeared as a guest on November 11, 1945. The discovery information had already been declassified (i.e., removed from the "Secret" category) for presentation at an American Chemical Society symposium at Northwestern University in Chicago the following Friday. Therefore, when one of the youngsters asked—during a session in which the author was trying to answer their questions—if any additional new elements had been discovered in the course of research on the nuclear weapon during the war, the author was able to reveal the existence of the elements 95 and 96. Apparently many children in America told their teachers about it the next day and, judging from some of the letters which the author subsequently received from such youngsters, they were not entirely successful in convincing their teachers. The formal announcement of the discoveries was, of course, made later, as planned.

FIGURE 6. *Photograph of an early hydroxide precipitation of americium, isolated in 1945 (magnified approximately nine times). The americium, in the form of the isotope americium-241, can be seen at the bottom of a solution in the capillary tube. An ordinary sewing needle is shown below the capillary tube for purposes of comparison.*

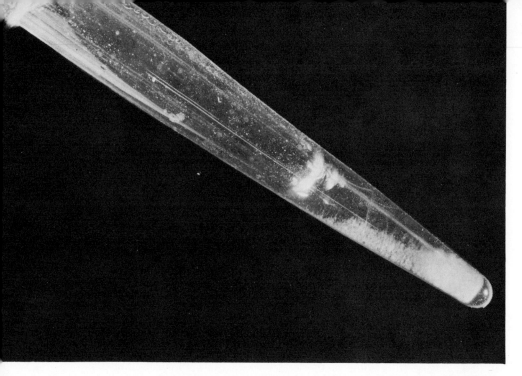

FIGURE 7. *Photograph of the first curium compound isolated in 1947 (magnified approximately two-and-one-half times). The compound is curium hydroxide, and the curium is in the form of the isotope curium-242. The precipitation is distributed throughout the solution in the capillary tube.*

Americium was first isolated by B.B. Cunningham, as the isotope americium-241, in the form of a pure compound, the hydroxide, in the fall of 1945 at the wartime Metallurgical Laboratory. A photograph of an early hydroxide precipitate is shown in Figure 6. Curium was first isolated in the form of a pure compound, the hydroxide, of curium-242 (produced by the neutron irradiation of americium-241) by L.B. Werner and I. Perlman at the University of California during the fall of 1947. A photograph of this first hydroxide is shown at Figure 7.

Berkelium and Californium

The most important prerequisite to the process for making the trans-curium elements was the manufacture of sufficiently large amounts of americium and curium to serve as target material. Because of the intense radioactivity of americium and curium, even in milligram or submilligram amounts, it was necessary to develop extremely efficient chemical separation methods to isolate the new elements from the target materials. This large degree of separation was necessary to detect the very small amounts of radioactivity due to the new elements produced in the presence of the highly radioactive starting materials. The dangerous radioactivity of the source material also made it necessary to institute complicated remote control methods of operation to keep health hazards at a minimum.

These problems were solved and successful experiments were performed by the end of 1949 and the beginning of 1950. Americium for target material was prepared in milligram amounts by intense neutron bombardment of plutonium over a long period of time, and curium target materials were prepared in microgram amounts as the result of the intense neutron bombardment of some of this americium. Both of these neutron bombardments took place in *high-flux reactors* (i.e., reactors that deliver large concentrations of neutrons that can be used for transmutation purposes).

Element 97 was discovered by S.G. Thompson, A. Ghiorso, and the author, in December, 1949, as a result of the bombardment of the milligram amounts of americium-241 with 35-Mev helium ions accelerated in the 60-inch cyclotron at Berkeley. The first isotope produced has the mass number 243 and decays primarily by orbital electron capture, with a half-life of 4.5 hours:

$$_{95}Am^{241} + {}_2He^4 \longrightarrow {}_{97}Bk^{243} \ (T_{\frac{1}{2}} = 4.5 \ h) + 2_0n^1$$

Element 98 was first produced and identified similarly by S.G. Thompson, K. Street, Jr., A. Ghiorso, and the author, in February of 1950, again at Berkeley. The first isotope produced is now assigned the mass number 245 and decays by alpha-particle emission and orbital electron capture with a half-life of 44 minutes. This isotope was produced by the bombardment of microgram amounts of curium-242 with 35-Mev helium ions accelerated in the 60-inch cyclotron:

$$_{96}Cm^{242} + {}_2He^4 \longrightarrow {}_{98}Cf^{245} \ (T_{\frac{1}{2}} = 44 \ m) + {}_0n^1$$

It is interesting to note that this identification of element 98 was accomplished with a total of only some 5,000 atoms; someone remarked at the time that this number was substantially smaller than the number of students attending the University of California.

The key to the discovery of these elements was the chemical identification by the ion-exchange adsorption and elution technique described in Chapter 4. The original data corresponding to these identifications are shown in Figures 8 and 9, for elements 97 and 98, respectively. Chapter 4 includes an explanation of the meaning of the curves and of the reference to Dowex-50 resin and eluting agent in the captions of Figures 8 and 9.

In the case of element 97, preliminary separations from the target americium were made by a procedure that involved the difficult oxidation of the americium to the VI state, the fluoride-soluble form, from which the element 97 was separated by coprecipitation with rare-earth fluoride. Preliminary separation of the element 98 from the target curium was effected by the ion-exchange adsorption-elution procedure. It can be seen that these elements elute in the expected order ahead of curium, and this constitutes convincing evidence for their chemical identification. The adsorption-elution experiment corresponding to the discovery of element 97 took place on December 19, 1949; that for element 98, on February 9, 1950.

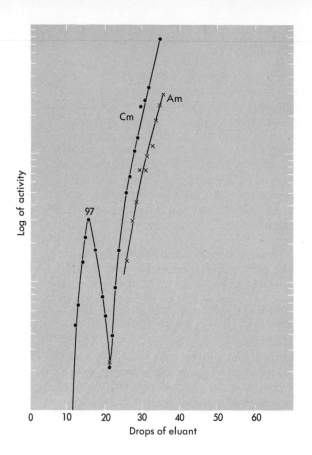

FIGURE 8. *Original elution data corresponding to the discovery of berkelium, December 19, 1949. Other activities were added for calibration purposes. Activity due to conversion electrons (Bk) and alpha particles (Cm and Am). (Dowex-50 resin at 87°C with ammonium citrate as eluting agent.)*

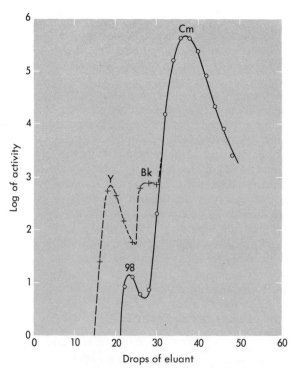

FIGURE 9. *Original elution data corresponding to the discovery of californium, February 9, 1950. Other activities were added for calibration purposes. Solid curve indicates alpha-particle counts / minute; dashed curve, conversion electrons and beta particles. (Dowex-50 resin at 87°C with ammonium citrate as eluting agent.)*

The story of the naming of elements 97 and 98 is an interesting one. Element 97 was called berkelium after the city of Berkeley, California, where it was discovered, just as its rare-earth analogue, terbium, was given a name derived from Ytterby, Sweden, where so many of the early rare-earth minerals were found. Element 98 was named californium, after the university and state where the work was done. This latter name, chosen for the reason given, does not reflect the observed chemical analogy of element 98 to dysprosium, as "americium," "curium," and "berkelium" signify that these elements are the chemical analogues of europium, gadolinium, and terbium, respectively. In their announcement of the discovery of element 98 in *Physical Review,* the authors commented, "The best we can do is point out, in recognition of the fact that dysprosium is named on the basis of a Greek word meaning 'difficult to get at,' that the searchers for another element a century ago found it difficult to get to California."

Upon learning about the naming of these elements, the "Talk of the Town" section of the *New Yorker* magazine had the following to say:

> New atoms are turning up with spectacular, if not downright alarming, frequency nowadays, and the University of California at Berkeley, whose scientists have discovered elements 97 and 98, has christened them berkelium and californium, respectively. While unarguably suited to their place of birth, these names strike us as indicating a surprising lack of public-relations foresight on the part of the university, located, as it is, in a state where publicity has flourished to a degree matched perhaps only by evangelism. California's busy scientists will undoubtedly come up with another atom or two one of these days, and the university might well have anticipated that. Now it has lost forever the chance of immortalizing itself in the atomic tables with some such sequence as universitium (97), ofium (98), californium (99), berkelium (100).

The discoverers sent the following reply:

> "Talk of the Town" has missed the point in their comments on naming of the elements 97 and 98. We may have shown lack of confidence but no lack of foresight in naming these elements "berkelium" and "californium." By using these names first, we have forestalled the appalling possibility that after naming 97 and 98 "universitium" and "ofium," some New Yorker might follow with the discovery of 99 and 100 and apply the names "newium" and "yorkium."

The answer from the *New Yorker* staff was brief:

> We are already at work in our office laboratories on "newium" and "yorkium." So far we just have the names.

In 1958, B.B. Cunningham and S.G. Thompson, at Berkeley, succeeded in isolating, for the first time, macroscopic amounts of berkelium as the isotope berkelium-249, and californium as a mixture of the isotopes californium-249, -250, -251, and -252. These were synthesized by the long-term irradiation of plutonium-239 and its transmutation products with neutrons in the Materials Testing Reactor at the National Reactor Testing Station in Idaho (described in Chapter 7).

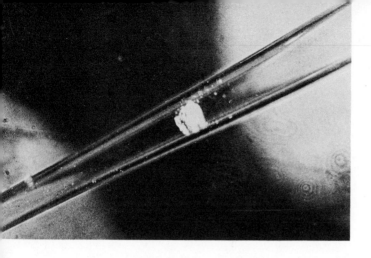

FIGURE 10. *Photograph of the first pure californium compound isolated in 1960, magnified about seventy times (0.3 micrograms of californium as the oxychloride, CfOCl). The californium was in the form of the isotope Cf²⁴⁹. The crystals are lodged in a capillary tube.*

The first compound of californium of proven molecular structure (by means of X-ray diffraction) was isolated in 1960 by Cunningham and J.C. Wallmann as three-tenths of a microgram of californium (as californium-249) oxychloride. The pure oxide and the trichloride were also prepared at that time. A photograph of the first such pure californium compound isolated appears at Figure 10. This experimental work was carried out on a *submicrogram* scale as the result of the further development of ultra-microchemical techniques. Figure 11 schematically shows some of the chemistry performed with this extremely minute quantity of californium.

The first compound of berkelium of proven molecular structure was isolated in 1962 by Cunningham and Wallmann. They isolated about 0.02

FIGURE 11. *Experimental setup for preparation of heavy element compounds, as for example those of californium, on the submicrogram scale.*

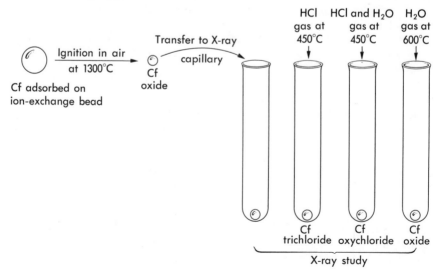

microgram of berkelium (as berkelium-249) dioxide and used about one-tenth of this, about 0.002 microgram (i.e., 2 nanograms), for the determination of its molecular structure by means of the X-ray diffraction technique.

Einsteinium and Fermium

The discovery of elements 99 and 100 represents an outstanding example of the unexpected in science. The seventh and eighth transuranium elements were discovered in debris from the "Mike" thermonuclear explosion which took place in the Pacific on November 1, 1952. This was the first large test of a thermonuclear device. Debris from the explosion was collected, first on filter papers attached to airplanes which flew through the clouds and, later in more substantial quantity, gathered up as fall-out material from the surface of a neighboring atoll. This debris was brought to the United States for chemical investigation in a number of laboratories.

Initial investigation at the Argonne National Laboratory in Chicago and at the Los Alamos Scientific Laboratory of the University of California in New Mexico led to the unexpected observation of heavy isotopes such as plutonium-244 and plutonium-246. At that time, the heaviest known isotope of plutonium was plutonium-243. Since this observation pointed to the capture of many successive neutrons by the uranium-238 in the device and thus the presence of neutron-excess isotopes in greater abundance than expected, a group at the University of California Radiation Laboratory undertook to look for isotopes of transcalifornium elements in this material. Figure 12 shows schematically the successive neutron captures that produced these neutron-excess isotopes. The successive, instantaneous capture of many neutrons by uranium-238 (in a time-scale of the order of microseconds) led to heavy uranium isotopes, as described in more detail in Chapter 7. In the summary table in the Appendix, these reactions are described by the notation "U^{238} multiple neutron capture." The heavy uranium isotopes decayed into the isotopes above them by the emission of negative beta particles.

Ion-exchange experiments of the type previously mentioned in the case of berkelium and californium (and described in more detail in Chapter 4) immediately demonstrated the existence of a new element. Later, in order to secure a larger amount of source material, it was necessary to process many hundreds of pounds of coral from one of the atolls adjoining the explosion area. Eventually, such coral was processed by the ton, using bismuth phosphate as the carrier for the tripositive actinide elements, in a pilot-plant operation which went under the name of "Paydirt."

Without going into the details, it may be pointed out that such experiments involving the groups at the three laboratories led to the positive identification of isotopes of elements 99 and 100. A twenty-day activity emitting alpha particles of 6.6-Mev energy was identified as an isotope of element 99 (with the mass number 253), and a 7.1-Mev alpha activity

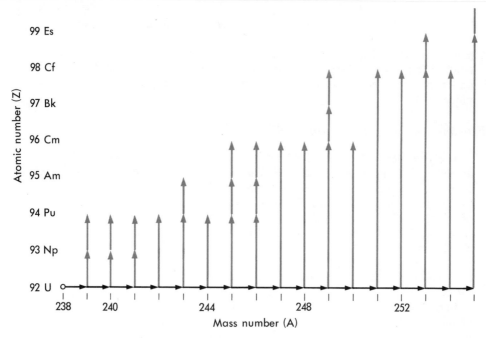

FIGURE 12. *Nuclear reactions for the synthesis of einsteinium and fermium in the first test thermonuclear explosion. Each neutron capture (horizontal arrows) adds one mass unit, and each beta decay (vertical arrows) increases the atomic number by one, while leaving the mass number unchanged.*

of twenty-two hours' half-life was identified as an isotope of element 100 (with the mass number 255).

The original ion-exchange adsorption-elution data for element 99, as recorded at Berkeley during the night of December 19, 1952, when this element was discovered, are shown in Figure 13, which again relies on Chapter 4 for an explanation of the meaning of the curves and of the reference to Dowex-50 resin and the eluting agent in the caption.

Similarly, the elution data recorded on March 1, 1953, for element 100, are plotted in Figure 14.

This experiment followed the initial discovery elution experiment, which took place at Berkeley on January 16, 1953, with such a small amount of element 100 that it was not possible to make the usual plot of a complete elution curve. This first identification of element 100 was made with only about 200 atoms. The most striking previous accomplishment in this category was the positive identification of element 98 with a total of about 5000 atoms.

The large group of scientists who contributed to the discovery of elements 99 and 100 included A. Ghiorso, S.G. Thompson, G.H. Higgins, and the author, of the Radiation Laboratory and Department of Chemistry of the University of California; M.H. Studier, P.R. Fields, S.M. Fried,

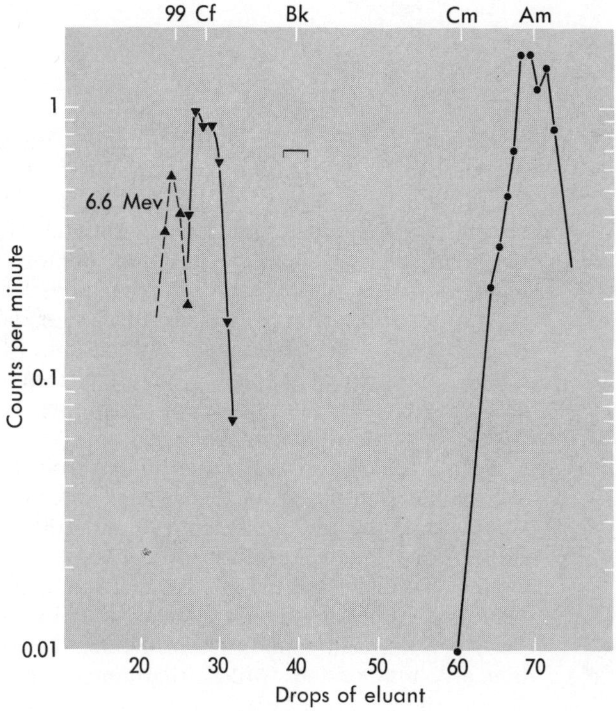

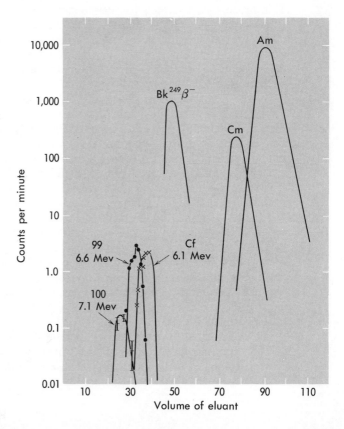

FIGURE 13. *Original elution data corresponding to discovery of einsteinium, December 19, 1952. Other activities were added for calibration purposes. Activity due to alpha particles. (Dowex-50 resin at 87°C with ammonium citrate as eluting agent.)*

FIGURE 14. *Elution data for fermium corresponding to second chemical identification, March 1, 1953. Other activities were added for calibration purposes. Activity, except for Bk^{249}, due to alpha particles. (Dowex-50 resin at 87 C with ammonium citrate as eluting agent.)*

H. Diamond, J.F. Mech, G.L. Pyle, J.R. Huizenga, A. Hirsch, and W.M. Manning of the Argonne National Laboratory; and C.I. Browne, H.L. Smith, and R.W. Spence of the Los Alamos Scientific Laboratory. These researchers suggested the name einsteinium for element 99 in honor of the great physicist, Albert Einstein; and for element 100, the name fermium in honor of the father of the atomic age, Enrico Fermi. The investigators also suggested the chemical symbols E for einsteinium and Fm for fermium. The Commission on Atomic Weights of the International Union of Pure and Applied Chemistry, responsible for the nomenclature of these elements, did not accept the proposed symbol for einsteinium and instead suggested the symbol Es.

Before removal of the "secret" label from this information and the subsequent announcement of the original discovery experiments could be accomplished, isotopes of elements 99 and 100 were produced by other, more conventional methods. Chief among these was that of successive neutron capture as the result of intense neutron irradiation of plutonium in the high-flux Materials Testing Reactor (MTR) at the National Reactor Testing Station in Idaho. The difference between this method of production and that of the "Mike" thermonuclear explosion is one of time as well as of starting material. In a reactor, it is necessary to bombard gram quantities of plutonium for two or three years; thus, the short-lived, intermediate isotopes of the various elements have an opportunity to decay. This process is described in more detail in Chapter 7 and is represented in the table in the Appendix by the notation "Pu^{239} multiple neutron capture." In the thermonuclear device, larger amounts of uranium were subjected to an extremely high neutron flux for a period of microseconds; the subsequent beta decay of the ultraheavy isotopes of uranium led to the nuclides found in the debris.

It was not until 1961 that sufficient einsteinium had been produced through intense neutron bombardments of plutonium-239 in the Materials Testing Reactor (described in Chapter 7) to permit separation of a macroscopic and weighable amount. B.B. Cunningham, J.C. Wallmann, L. Phillips, and R.C. Gatti, working on the submicrogram scale, were able to separate a small fraction of pure einsteinium-253. This was a remarkable feat, since the total amount of material involved was only a few hundredths of a microgram of einsteinium. As was true with all other isolations of weighable quantities of the transuranium elements, it was possible to observe a macroscopic property—in this case, the magnetic susceptibility of einsteinium.

Fermium has not been separated in weighable amounts to date and, because of the short half-lives of its isotopes, it will be a very long time before this extremely difficult task is considered worthwhile.

Mendelevium

The discovery of this element was, in many ways, the most dramatic. It was decided to make an attempt at discovery in a situation which might be regarded as very premature. All previous discoveries of transuranium elements had begun with weighable amounts of target materials. It was thought, however, that techniques had advanced to a point where it might be possible to identify element 101 as a transmutation product produced in a target so small that it was unweighable.

The plan of attack required the bombardment of the maximum quantity of einsteinium available, in the form of the isotope einsteinium-253, with 40-Mev helium ions in the Berkeley 60-inch cyclotron. It was found that the available einsteinium-253 produced in the Materials Testing Reactor totalled only about 10^9, or one billion, atoms. To assay the possibilities, the number of atoms of element 101 which reasonably could be expected to arise from the bombardment could be deduced from the following simple considerations. The number of atoms, N, of element 101 should be given approximately by the following expression

$$N \cong N' \sigma I t$$

where N' designates the number of einsteinium atoms used as a target; σ, the cross section or probability for the reaction; I, the intensity of the helium ion beam; and t, the effective time of the bombardment. The cross section, σ, could be predicted to be about 10^{-27} cm^2 on the basis of the known values for previously-observed similar reactions in this region. (The concept of nuclear cross section is discussed in Chapter 10.) As a result of certain fundamental changes in the cyclotron, made to increase the intensity of the helium-ion beam to a value higher than ever before attained, it was possible to attain 100 microamperes per cm^2, or about 10^{14} particles/sec/cm^2 for I. Predictions for the half-life of the expected isotopes suggested the range of hours, so that an effective time of bombardment of about 10^4 seconds was all that would be useful. Calculation based on these data is:

$$N \cong N' \sigma I t \cong (10^9)\ (10^{-27})\ (10^{14})\ (10^4) \cong 1 \text{ atom}$$

Thus, the production of only one atom of element 101 per experiment could be expected!

Adding immeasurably to the complexity of the experiment was the absolute necessity for the chemical separation of the one atom of element 101 from the 10^9 atoms of einsteinium in the target and its ultimate, complete chemical identification by separation with the now familiar ion-exchange method. This separation and identification would presumably have to take place in a period of hours, or perhaps even one hour or less, because the expected half-life was of this order of magnitude.

These requirements indicated the desperate need for new techniques, together with some luck. Fortunately, both were forthcoming. The new technique involved separation of the element 101 by the recoil method from the einsteinium in the target. The einsteinium was placed on a gold foil in an invisibly thin layer. The helium-ion beam was sent through the back of the foil so that the atoms of element 101, recoiling through a vacuum due to the momentum of the impinging helium ions, could be caught on a second thin, gold catcher foil—as shown in Figure 15. This second gold foil, which contained recoil atoms and was relatively free of the einsteinium target material, was dissolved and was used for later chemical operations.

The earliest experiments were confined to a search for short-lived, alpha-emitting isotopes that might be due to element 101. For this purpose, it was sufficient to look quickly at the actinide chemical fraction as separated by the ion-exchange method. No alpha activity was observed that could be attributed to element 101, even when the time between the end of bombardment and the be-ginning of the alpha particle analyses had been reduced to five minutes.

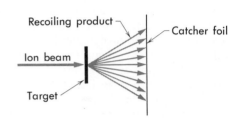

FIGURE 15. *The recoil technique.*

The experiments were continued and, in one of the subsequent bombard-ments, a single, large pulse in the electronic detection apparatus due to spontaneous fission was observed. With probably unjustified self-confidence, it was thought that this might be a significant result. Although such an attitude might ordinarily have been considered foolish, it must be recalled that rapid decay by spontaneous fission was—up until that time—con-fined to only a few isotopes, none of which should have been introduced spuriously into the experiment. In addition, background counts due to this mode of decay should be essentially zero in proper equipment.

The major question, of course, was whether the experiment could be repeated. In a number of subsequent bombardments, one or two spon-taneous fission events were observed in some, while none was observed in other experiments. This, of course, was to be expected, because of the statistical fluctuation inherent in the production of the order of one atom per bombardment. Furthermore, more advanced chemical experi-ments seemed to indicate that spontaneous fission counts, when they did appear, came in about the element 100 or 101 chemical fractions. At about this time, a fire-bell was hung in the chemistry building, connected to the counting circuit so that a loud "clang" rang out each time one of these rare spontaneous fission events registered. This sport was put to a justifiable end when it came to the attention of the fire department!

The definitive experiments were performed in a memorable, all-night session, February 18, 1955. To increase the number of events that might be observed at one time, three successive three-hour bombardments were made, and, in turn, their transmutation products were quickly and com-pletely separated by the ion-exchange method. Some of the isotope ein-steinium-253 was present in each case so that, together with the cali-fornium-246 produced from curium-244 also present in the target, it was possible to define the positions in which the elements came off the column used to contain the ion-exchange resin. Five spontaneous fission counters then were used to count simultaneously the corresponding drops of solution from the three runs.

A total of five spontaneous fission counts were observed in the element 101 position, while a total of eight spontaneous fission counts were also observed in the element 100 position. No such counts were observed in any other position. The original data are presented in Figures 16 and 17. The interpretation of Figure 16 again relies on the explanation of the ion-exchange adsorption-elution method given in Chapter 4.

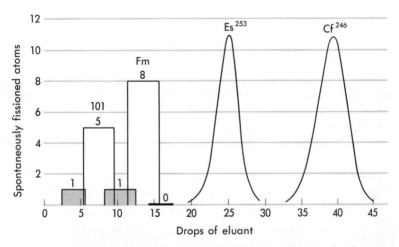

FIGURE 16. *Original elution data corresponding to the discovery of mendelevium, February 18, 1955. The curves for einsteinium-253 and californium-246 are for alpha-particle emissions. (Dowex-50 ion-exchange resin was used, and the eluting agent was ammonium alpha-hydroxyisobutyrate).*

The rate of spontaneous fission in both the element 101 and 100 fractions decayed with a half-life of about three hours (later determined to be 160 minutes). This and other evidence led to the hypothesis that this isotope of element 101 has the mass number 256 and decays, by orbital electron capture (designated by the symbol E.C.) with a half-life of the order of one-and-one-half hours, to the isotope fermium-256, which is responsible for the spontaneous fission decay. The discovery reactions are:

$$_{99}Es^{253} + _{2}He^{4} \longrightarrow _{101}Md^{256} + _{0}n^{1}$$

$$_{101}Md^{256} \xrightarrow[\ T_{1/2} = \sim 1.5\ h\ ]{E.C.} {}_{100}Fm^{256}$$

$$_{100}Fm^{256} \xrightarrow[\ T_{1/2} = \sim 160\ m\ ]{} \text{spontaneous fission}$$

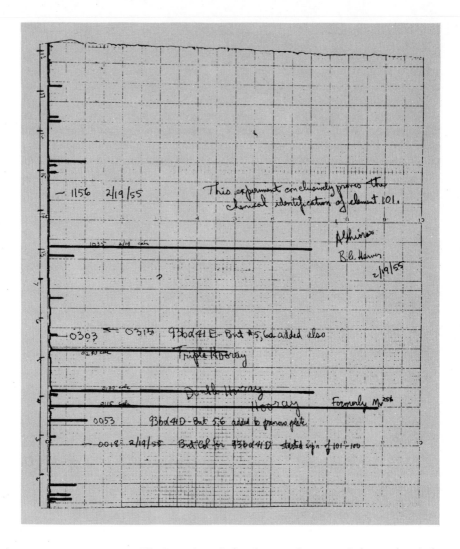

FIGURE 17. *A portion of the chart used to record the results of the fission counters in the discovery experiments for mendelevium.*

On the basis of this evidence, the group, consisting of A. Ghiorso, B.G. Harvey, G.R. Choppin, S.G. Thompson, and the author, announced to the world the discovery of element 101. The name mendelevium was suggested, in recognition of the pioneering role of the great Russian chemist, Dmitri Mendeleev, who was the first to use the periodic system of the elements to predict the chemical properties of undiscovered elements, a principle which has been the key to the discovery of nearly all of the transuranium elements. As was the case with einsteinium, the symbol Mv for mendelevium, proposed by the investigators, was not accepted by the international body responsible for nomenclature, and instead Md has been suggested.

It is comforting to be able to record that subsequent experiments using larger amounts of einsteinium in the target have led to the production of thousands of atoms of mendelevium, lending confirmation to the sparse evidence on which the original conclusions were made. The indications are that, as expected, mendelevium is a typical tripositive actinide element.

Element 102

In 1957, a team of scientists from Argonne National Laboratory in the United States, the Atomic Energy Research Establishment in England, and the Nobel Institute for Physics in Sweden, announced the discovery of an isotope of element 102 as a result of research performed at the Nobel Institute for Physics in Stockholm.

The isotope was reportedly produced by bombarding curium-244 with cyclotron-produced carbon-13 ions having a charge of $+4$. On the basis of only a few events, the group reported the isotope as decaying by the emission of 8.5 Mev alpha-particles with a half-life of about 10 minutes. The name nobelium was suggested by this group for the supposedly new element, in honor and in recognition of Alfred Nobel's contributions to the advancement of science; this name was accepted prematurely by the Commission on Atomic Weights of the International Union of Pure and Applied Chemistry.

However, neither experiments with the facilities at the University of California in Berkeley, nor related experiments performed in the U.S.S.R., have confirmed this Stockholm work. The Berkeley attempts at confirmation were quite extensive and, since these experiments were more sensitive than the Stockholm experiments, seem to be conclusive in their rejection of the earlier results. The Soviet studies were conducted by G.N. Flerov and co-workers at the Atomic Energy Institute.

In 1958, a group at the University of California reported the positive identification of the isotope of element 102 with the mass number 254 as a product of the bombardment of curium-246 with carbon-12 ions accelerated in the then new heavy ion linear accelerator (HILAC) at Berkeley:

$$_{96}Cm^{246} + {}_6C^{12} \longrightarrow 102^{254} + 4_0n^1$$

$$102^{254} \xrightarrow[\textstyle T_{1/2} = \sim 3 \text{ s}]{} {}_{100}Fm^{250} + {}_2He^4$$

This is designated in the short-hand notation as the $(C^{12}, 4n)$ reaction.

The new element was detected by the chemical identification (through the ion-exchange method) of its known daughter, fermium-250, which decays by the emission of 7.43-Mev alpha-particles with a half-life of 30 minutes. The removal of the element 102 isotope from the target material, and the separation of the daughter element from the parent element 102, were performed by the use of a new method involving two physical separations.

This experiment bears resemblance to that of the discovery of mendelevium, except that the half-lives involved were even shorter, necessitating more sophisticated techniques. These are indicated in Figure 18, which is a schematic drawing of the experimental arrangement:

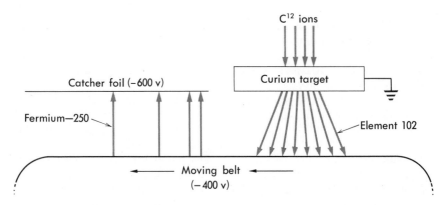

FIGURE 18. *The experimental arrangement used in the discovery of element 102.*

Here, again, the amount involved required identification of the new element, atom by atom. The target, consisting of a mixture of curium isotopes deposited on a thin nickel foil, was enclosed in a container filled with helium gas. The curium was bombarded with carbon-12 ions, and the transmuted atoms were knocked into the helium gas to absorb their recoil energy. With a sufficient electric field strength, it was found that nearly all of these positively-charged atoms could be attracted to a moving, negatively-charged metallic belt placed directly beneath the target. The belt was then passed under a foil (the catcher foil) which was charged negatively relative to the belt. Approximately half of the element 102 atoms undergoing radioactive decay by alpha-particle emission caused their daughter atoms to recoil from the surface of the belt to the catcher foil.

The catcher foil was cut transversely to the direction of the belt motion into five equal-length sections, after a bombardment of about one hour. Each section then was analyzed simultaneously in alpha-particle energy analyzers. Thus, all of the desired measurements could be made for identifying the daughter atoms caught on the catcher foils and the half-life of the parent of the recoiling atoms could be determined. Figure 19 shows the elution data obtained during the discovery experiments. Again, the interpretation of these data relies on the description of the ion-exchange adsorption-elution method given in Chapter 4.

It was found that fermium-250 could be collected on the catcher foil in accordance with a parent half-life (i.e., half-life for 102^{254}) of three seconds. Changing the belt speed was found to change the distribution of the fermium-250 on the catcher foil in a manner conforming to a three-second parent. The variation of the yield of the three-second activity with the energy of the carbon-12 ions was also consistent with that expected for a (C^{12}, 4n) reaction.

In experiments starting in 1957 and continuing through 1958, G.N. Flerov and co-workers in Moscow produced a nuclide or nuclides emitting 8.8 ± 0.5-Mev alpha-particles, with half-life in the range of five to twenty seconds, in the bombardment of plutonium-241 (and plutonium-242) with high energy oxygen-16 ions accelerated in a cyclotron. This product was separated from the target by the recoil technique, and the energy of the alpha particles was approximately measured by the use of a photographic emulsion technique. No chemical identification was possible. It is possible that this activity is due to the isotope of element 102 with the mass number 253.

In later experiments at Berkeley, the recoil atoms of element 102 were caught on a belt which was quickly pulled inside an alpha-particle counter in order to measure directly the energy of the alpha particles and the half-life of the isotope with mass number 254. The values of 8.3-Mev for the energy of the alpha particles, and three seconds for the half-life, were obtained.

Although the name nobelium for element 102 undoubtedly will have to be changed, no suggestion for a new name has yet been made. This probably will not be done until more evidence or confirmation of the results is obtained.

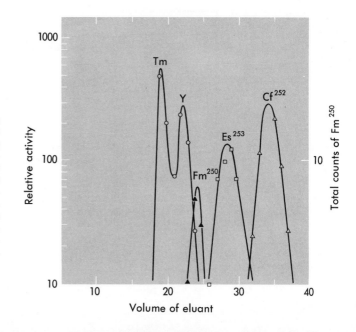

FIGURE 19. *Elution data obtained in the discovery of element 102, showing the presence of fermium-250—the decay product of 102^{254}. Other activities were added for calibration purposes. (Dowex-50 ion-exchange resin was used, and the eluting agent was ammonium alpha-hydroxyisobutyrate).*

Lawrencium

In the spring of 1961, following almost three years of work begun shortly after the discovery of element 102, a group at Berkeley—A. Ghiorso, T. Sikkeland, A.E. Larsh, and R.M. Latimer—produced and identified an isotope of element 103. The discoverers suggested the name lawrencium in honor of the late Ernest O. Lawrence, inventor of the cyclotron and founder and longtime director of the Radiation Laboratory at Berkeley.

The method used to produce and identify lawrencium is similar to that used in the discovery of element 102, as shown in Figure 20.

Three micrograms of a mixture of californium isotopes (mass numbers 249, 250, 251, and 252) were periodically bombarded with a heavy ion beam of boron-10 and -11 in the HILAC (the heavy-ion linear accelerator) at Berkeley. Using californium-252, for example—the discovery reactions were:

$$_{98}\text{Cf}^{252} + {}_5\text{B}^{11} \longrightarrow {}_{103}\text{Lw}^{257} \ (T_{\frac{1}{2}} = {\sim}8 \text{ s}) + 6_0\text{n}^1$$

$$_{98}\text{Cf}^{252} + {}_5\text{B}^{10} \longrightarrow {}_{103}\text{Lw}^{257} \ (T_{\frac{1}{2}} = {\sim}8 \text{ s}) + 5_0\text{n}^1$$

The atoms of lawrencium recoiled from the target into an atmosphere of helium and were then electrostatically collected on a copper-coated plastic tape. This tape was automatically placed before radiation detectors every few seconds to measure the emission rate and the energy of the alpha particles being emitted.

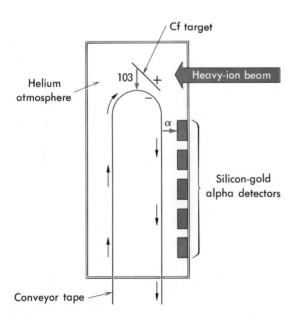

FIGURE 20. *Experimental apparatus used to detect element 103, lawrencium. The transmuted atoms were electrically attracted to a movable copper-coated plastic tape. This conveyed the atoms to specially made silicon-gold detectors that could analyze the energy of the alpha particles emitted.*

Table 2   THE TRANSURANIUM ELEMENTS

Atomic Number	Element	Symbol	Atomic Weight[a]	Discoverers and Date of Discovery	Source of First Preparation	First Isolation in Weighable Amount
93	neptunium	Np	237	E.M. McMillan and P.H. Abelson, 1940	Irradiation of uranium with neutrons	1944 Np^{237} (2.2×10^6 y), L.B. Magnusson and T.J. LaChapelle
94	plutonium	Pu	242	G.T. Seaborg, E.M. McMillan, J.W. Kennedy, and A.C. Wahl, 1940–41	Bombardment of uranium with deuterons	1942 Pu^{239} (24,360 y), B.B. Cunningham and L.B. Werner
95	americium	Am	243	G.T. Seaborg, R.A. James, L.O. Morgan, and A. Ghiorso, 1944–45	Irradiation of plutonium with neutrons	1945 Am^{241} (458 y), B.B. Cunningham
96	curium	Cm	248	G.T. Seaborg, R.A. James, and A. Ghiorso, 1944	Bombardment of plutonium with helium ions	1947 Cm^{242} (162.5 d), L.B. Werner and I. Perlman
97	berkelium	Bk	249	S.G. Thompson, A. Ghiorso, and G.T. Seaborg, 1949	Bombardment of americium with helium ions	1958 Bk^{249} (314 d), S.G. Thompson and B.B. Cunningham
98	californium	Cf	249	S.G. Thompson, K. Street, Jr., A. Ghiorso, and G.T. Seaborg, 1950	Bombardment of curium with helium ions	1958 $Cf^{249-252}$, B.B. Cunningham and S.G. Thompson
99	einsteinium	Es	254	A. Ghiorso, S.G. Thompson, G.H. Higgins, G.T. Seaborg, M.H. Studier, P.R. Fields, S.M. Fried, H. Diamond, J.F. Mech, G.L. Pyle, J.R. Huizenga, A. Hirsch, W.M. Manning, C.I. Browne, H.L. Smith, and R.W. Spence, 1952	Irradiation of uranium with neutrons in first thermonuclear explosion	1961 Es^{253} (20 d), B.B. Cunningham, J.C. Wallmann, L. Phillips, and R.C. Gatti
100	fermium	Fm	253	(same as einsteinium), 1953	In first thermonuclear explosion	
101	mendelevium	Md	256	A. Ghiorso, B.G. Harvey, G.R. Choppin, S.G. Thompson, and G.T. Seaborg, 1955	Bombardment of einsteinium with helium ions	
102	—	—	254	A. Ghiorso, T. Sikkeland, J.R. Walton, and G.T. Seaborg, 1958	Bombardment of curium with carbon ions	
103	lawrencium	Lw	257	A. Ghiorso, T. Sikkeland, A.E. Larsh, and R.M. Latimer, 1961	Bombardment of californium with boron ions	

[a] Mass number of longest lived or more available isotope.   y = years.   d = days.

By this means, it was possible to identify the lawrencium isotope, with a mass number of 257 and a half-life of approximately eight seconds, which decays through the emission of alpha particles with an energy of 8.6 Mev. The eight-second activity was assigned to lawrencium-257 because the variation of its yield with the energy of the boron-10 and -11 ions was as expected for the production of lawrencium-257; also, the yield of this activity, resulting from the bombardment of californium with other ions such as carbon-12 ions, was found to be consistent with that expected on the basis of known reaction yields. Experiments were made with various other target elements to show that the new activity was produced only with the californium target. These "background" experiments were found to be particularly important because it was discovered that superficially similar activities could be produced by heavy-ion bombardment of lead and bismuth target impurities.

At present, because of the short half-life of lawrencium, it has not been possible to perform a chemical identification, and the discovery rests solely on nuclear evidence.

Summary

The historical facts associated with the discovery of the transuranium elements are summarized in Table 2. It should be noted that the heaviest elements have not been, and possibly never will be, isolated in visible amounts because of the ever-decreasing stabilities and half-lives. Einsteinium (the 250-day Es^{254}, or the 20-day Es^{253}) may be the last transuranium element that can be physically weighed.

The Appendix contains a complete listing of the known isotopes of these transuranium elements. It includes their half-lives, mode of decay, summary details of the decay process, and methods of production.

3

Position

in the Periodic

Table

Prior to the Discovery
of the Transuranium Elements

During the eighteenth century, about a dozen new chemical elements were discovered, and the atomic theory of matter was born. About 60 more elements were identified in the nineteenth century. In the same period, Dmitri Mendeleev, the great Russian chemist, brought order out of the chaos about the elements with the perfection of his Periodic Table, giving us, at the same time, the tremendous advantage of being able to predict the properties of the then undiscovered elements.

The Periodic Table was soon elaborated to show positions for 92 elements. By the middle of the third decade of the present century, all 92 of these elements had been discovered, with the exception of those with the atomic numbers 43, 61, 85, and 87. Even these properly empty places in the Periodic Table were filled under names such as masurium for element 43, illinium for element 61, alabamine for element 85, and virginium for element 87. These "discoveries," however, were erroneous. The state of the understanding of the atomic nucleus was such in the 1930's that it could be shown that the missing elements were all radioactive, with such short half-lives that their existence in appreciable concentrations on the earth was not possible.

Figure 21 shows the Periodic Table as it looked before World War II, when scientists first tried to produce elements beyond uranium. Elements no. 43, technetium (Tc); no. 61, promethium (Pm); no. 85, astatine (At); and no. 87, francium (Fr), are included here, although they actually were given their names later, and some were first synthesized or discovered at a later date.

Thoughts on the position in the Periodic Table of the heaviest elements varied considerably before the final recognition that another series of elements resulting from the addition of electrons to an inner shell (5f) should occur somewhere in the heavy-element region. This new family of elements would be similar to the rare-earth or lanthanide (chemically similar to lanthanum) series of elements which result from the addition of inner 4f electrons. The designations 5f and 4f are a part of the nomenclature for describing the orbital and other properties of individual electrons (see Chapter 8). Thus, the "5" and "4" tell us that the electron is in the 5th or 4th major electron shell (measuring out from the nucleus), and the "f" identifies a particular subshell. These are inner shells because some electrons occupy positions as far out as the 7th and 6th major shells in the heaviest elements (7s shell) and the lanthanide elements (6s shell).

In the 1920's, lanthanum and the "rare-earth" elements were fitted between barium and hafnium, as indeed they are today. Even up until World War II, however, the three heaviest-known elements—thorium, protactinium, and uranium—were believed to be related to hafnium, tantalum, and tungsten, respectively. The next element—number 93—was thus expected to have chemical properties resembling those of rhenium. Similarly,

FIGURE 21. *Periodic Table before World War II. Atomic numbers of the then undiscovered transuranium elements range from 93 to 100.*

H																	He
Li	Be											B	C	N	O	F	Ne
Na	Mg											Al	Si	P	S	Cl	Ar
K	Ca	Sc	Ti	V	Cr	Mn	Fe	Co	Ni	Cu	Zn	Ga	Ge	As	Se	Br	Kr
Rb	Sr	Y	Zr	Nb	Mo	Tc	Ru	Rh	Pd	Ag	Cd	In	Sn	Sb	Te	I	Xe
Cs	Ba	La-Lu	Hf	Ta	W	Re	Os	Ir	Pt	Au	Hg	Tl	Pb	Bi	Po	At	Rn
Fr	Ra	Ac	Th	Pa	U	93	94	95	96	97	98	99	100				
		La	Ce	Pr	Nd	Pm	Sm	Eu	Gd	Tb	Dy	Ho	Er	Tm	Yb	Lu	

elements 94 to 100 were expected to fit into the Periodic Table in the manner shown in Figure 21.

The first attempts to produce elements beyond uranium were made by Fermi, Segrè, and co-workers, who bombarded uranium with neutrons in Italy in 1934 (see Chapter 2). They actually found a number of radioactive products. The radioactive products of the neutron bombardment of uranium were the object of chemical investigations during the following years by O. Hahn, L. Meitner, and F.S. Strassmann, in Germany, and by numerous other scientists. On the basis of incomplete tracer studies, some of these activities seemed to have chemical properties such as would be expected for "transuranium" elements with an atomic number such as 94 or 96—i.e., properties similar to those of elements such as osmium and platinum listed directly above elements 94 and 96 in the Periodic Table of that time (see Figure 21). Subsequent work—especially the discovery of nuclear fission by O. Hahn and F.S. Strassmann and their co-workers in 1938—showed that this interpretation was not correct. This subsequent work revealed that these products of the uranium bombardments actually were radioactive isotopes of lighter elements and were fission product elements such as barium, lanthanum, iodine, tellurium, or molybdenum.

Following the Discovery
of the Transuranium Elements

The discovery of an element with atomic number higher than 92 came in 1940 as the result of the work of E.M. McMillan and P.H. Abelson (see Chapter 2). This was followed shortly by the discovery of plutonium by the author, E.M. McMillan, J.W. Kennedy, and A.C. Wahl, in late 1940. The tracer chemical experiments with neptunium and plutonium showed that their chemical properties were much like those of uranium and not at all like those of rhenium and osmium.

For a few years following this, uranium, neptunium, and plutonium, were considered to be sort of "cousins" in the Periodic Table, but the family relationship was not clear. It was thought that elements 95 and 96 should be much like them in their chemical properties. Thus it was thought that these elements formed a "uranide" (chemically similar to uranium) group.

The Periodic Table of 1944, shown in Figure 22, therefore implied that the chemical properties of elements 95 and 96 should be very much like those of neptunium and plutonium. These assumptions proved to be wrong, and the experiments directed toward the discovery of elements 95 and 96 failed (see Chapter 2). Again, the undiscovered elements 95 and 96 apparently refused to fit the pattern indicated by the Periodic Table of 1944.

Then, in 1944, the author conceived the idea that perhaps all the known elements heavier than actinium were misplaced on the Periodic Table. The theory advanced was that these elements heavier than actinium might constitute a second series similar to the series of "rare-earth" or "lanthanide" elements. The lanthanides are chemically very similar to each other and

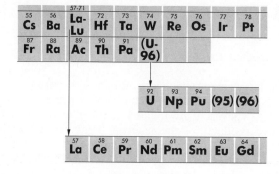

FIGURE 22. *The heavy elements' position in the Periodic Table in 1944. Atomic numbers of the then undiscovered elements are in parentheses.*

usually are listed in a separate row below the main part of the Periodic Table. This would mean that all these heavier elements really belonged with actinium—directly after radium in the Periodic Table—just as the known "lanthanides" fit in with lanthanum between barium (Ba) and hafnium (Hf).

The revised Periodic Table, then, listed the heaviest elements as a second "rare-earth" series. These heaviest elements (including undiscovered elements), with the name "actinide" elements, were paired off with those in the already-known lanthanide rare-earth series, as in Figure 23.

The new concept meant that elements 95 and 96 should have some properties in common with actinium and some in common with their rare-earth "sisters," europium and gadolinium, especially with respect to the difficulty of oxidation above the III state. When experiments were designed according to this new concept, elements 95 and 96 were soon discovered—that is, they were synthesized and chemically identified.

Since all the elements beyond actinium (through lawrencium, element 103) belong to the actinide group, the elements thorium, protactinium, and uranium, have been removed from the positions they occupied in the Periodic Table before World War II and placed in this transition family. Elements 104, 105, and 106, when discovered, will presumably take over the positions previously held by thorium, protactinium, and uranium. Thus we have the interesting result that the newcomers have affected the face of the Periodic Table, and a change has been made after many years even though it seemed to have assumed its final form.

The actinide elements are very similar to each other and to the lanthanides. The actinides generally have the following properties in common: trivalent cations which form complex ions and organic chelates; soluble

FIGURE 23. *The position of the actinide elements in the Periodic Table as predicted in 1944. Atomic numbers of the then undiscovered elements are in parentheses.*

57 La	58 Ce	59 Pr	60 Nd	61 Pm	62 Sm	63 Eu	64 Gd	65 Tb	66 Dy	67 Ho	68 Er	69 Tm	70 Yb	71 Lu
89 Ac	90 Th	91 Pa	92 U	93 Np	94 Pu	(95)	(96)	(97)	(98)	(99)	(100)	(101)	(102)	(103)

sulfates, nitrates, halides, perchlorates, and sulfides; and acid-insoluble fluorides and oxalates.

The early members of the actinide series have chemical properties related to those of the lanthanide elements, although quite different with respect to their oxidation-reduction behavior. The actinide elements lose electrons more easily in chemical reactions to form higher oxidation states, as is to be expected because of the looser binding of their inner (i.e., 5f shell) electrons (see Chapters 8 and 9). The later members of the actinide series are more chemically similar to their lanthanide counterparts.

The Periodic Table, as it is understood today, is shown in Figure 24. The undiscovered "transactinide" elements—i.e., the elements with atomic numbers greater than 103—have their atomic numbers in parentheses and are fitted into the Periodic Table as shown. Of course, not all of these elements will be discovered because their predicted half-lives decrease drastically with increasing atomic number, as will be described in Chapters 5 and 10.

FIGURE 24. *The Periodic Table of today. The atomic numbers of undiscovered elements are in parentheses.*

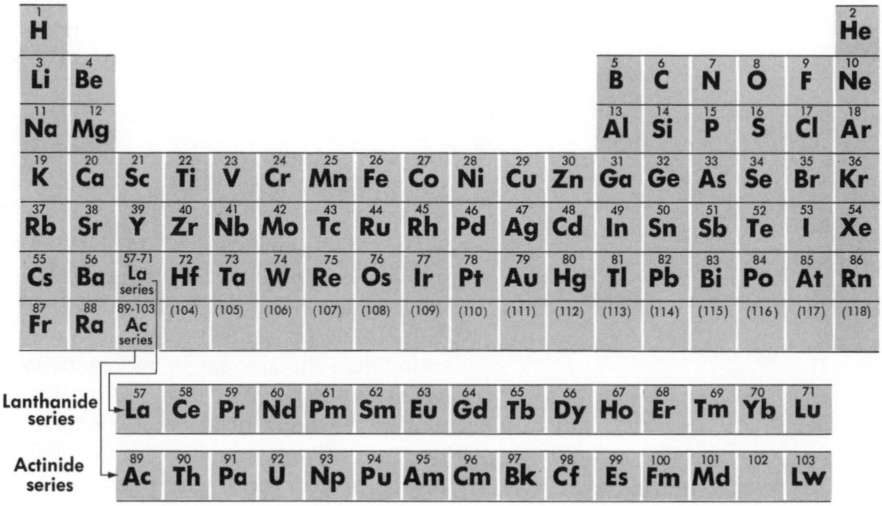

4

Experimental

Chemical Methods

of Investigation

This chapter summarizes some of the main chemical methods of experimental investigation of the transuranium elements and some of the problems associated with such investigations. Some of these experimental methods have been described in other chapters in connection with their application to the investigation of particular transuranium elements, and cross references to these discussions are made here.

Methods for Handling Radioactive Material

Special equipment and facilities to shield the experimenter against radiation are necessary for manipulation of the actinide elements on the laboratory scale when the amount of radioactivity is large. However, these protective measures are not needed for the small amounts of radioactivity that are usually employed for tracer experiments.

Enclosed containers (gloved boxes) are used for work with radioactive nuclides that emit nonpenetrating radiation (alpha particles) and that do not emit significant quantities of beta or gamma radiation. This is necessary in order to prevent ingestion of the radioactive nuclide by the laboratory worker and to prevent its spread throughout the laboratory. A photograph of a

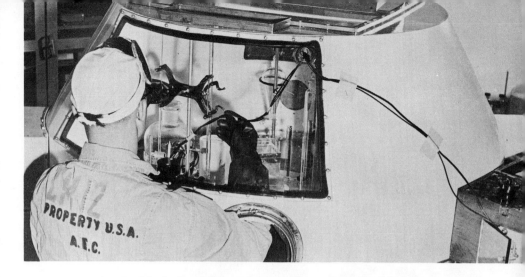

FIGURE 25. *A gloved box at the Los Alamos Scientific Laboratory is used to handle irradiated materials emitting weak particle radiation. Experimenters handle the material efficiently and safely with rubber gloves inside a ventilated cabinet.*

laboratory worker with such special equipment is shown in Figure 25.

Work with radioactive nuclides, either alpha- or beta-particle emitters, that give off penetrating radiation (gamma rays) is carried out by remote control behind shielding material such as lead. In some cases, enclosed containers with gloved portholes and heavy shielding material are used for work with radioactive nuclides, or mixtures of radioactive nuclides, that emit both alpha particles and moderate numbers of gamma rays. More intricate apparatus, such as the so-called "master-slave manipulators" and "hot cells" are used for remote control operations behind large thicknesses of shielding material when very large amounts of gamma ray emitters are handled. The apparatus is shown in Figure 26. The manipulation of nuclides that emit large numbers of neutrons, as the result of decay by spontaneous fission, is especially difficult and requires the interposition of neutron-slowing and -absorbing material.

Radiochemical Procedures

Investigations of radioactive materials are frequently carried out on the *tracer* scale, where a substance under examination is present in very low concentration, in much less than weighable amounts, and where its radioactivity offers a means for detecting its presence (see Chapter 2, under neptunium and plutonium). The course of the radioactive nuclide is traced through successive chemical procedures by measuring the amount of radioactivity in the various chemical fractions. Nonradioactive *carrier* material is used for precipitation processes; however, carrier material is not required in many chemical processes—as for example, the ion exchange processes described in Chapter 2 and in a later section in this chapter. The amount of material involved ranges from as little as one atom up to 10^{12} or more atoms (i.e., 10^{-9} or more grams).

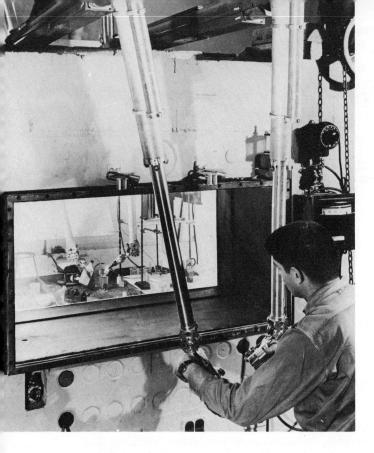

FIGURE 26. *A step in preparation of a solid sample of extremely radioactive material for analysis is concluded as the scientist, separated from his work by a concrete barrier and a liquid-filled porthole, uses master-slave manipulators, or "mechanical hands," to wash his equipment.*

Procedures such as those described here are, of course, applied to work with the heavier transcurium elements, where only a few score atoms may be available. These methods were used in the earliest work with all the transuranium elements and continue to be used with all of them to some extent to the present time. Tracer studies offer a method for obtaining rough knowledge of oxidation states, formation of complex ions, and the solubility of various compounds. These techniques, of course, are not applicable to other important fields of investigation, such as crystallography, metallurgy, and optical spectroscopy.

Properties of Nuclides Used in Chemical Investigations

The study of the chemical behavior of concentrated preparations of the shorter-lived nuclides available in macroscopic (weighable) quantities is made difficult in both aqueous solutions and in solid compounds by their high radioactivity per unit weight (i.e., high *specific activity*). In aqueous solutions, the radioactivity can rapidly dissociate water to produce hydrogen and hydrogen peroxide, and in solid compounds it can destroy the crystal lattices. Studies are complicated by the continuous heating of the sample (most of the radioactive decay energy is converted into heat) and by the rapid destruction of chemical bonds by the fast-moving decay particles. In addition, the sample quickly becomes contaminated by decay products. Studies of the metallic state are less affected by these difficulties because of the nonlocalized nature of metallic bonds.

Neptunium in the form of the isotope neptunium-237 is relatively safe and convenient to work with in chemical investigations. With respect to plutonium, most chemical investigations to date have been performed with the isotope plutonium-239, but the isotopes plutonium-242 and plutonium-244 are more suitable for such work because of their longer half-lives and consequently lower specific activity. The existence of very large quantities of the fissionable isotope plutonium-239 places emphasis upon the physiological toxicity of plutonium. In this form, plutonium is a dangerous poison because of its relatively high specific alpha radioactivity (1.4×10^8, or 140,000,000 alpha particles per minute per milligram) and its physiological behavior. Ingested plutonium may be transferred to the bone and, over a period of time, the alpha radiation associated with its decay gives rise to bone cancer and other neoplasms. The maximum permissible amount of plutonium-239 that can be safely lodged in the body is about one microgram, corresponding to about 100,000 alpha-particle disintegrations per minute. (Since one curie corresponds to 3.7×10^{10} disintegrations per second, this amount of plutonium-239 corresponds to about 0.05 microcuries.)

Nevertheless, work on plutonium can be carried out with complete safety, provided proper laboratory precautions are utilized. A curious hazard, which affects only fissionable isotopes, is the *criticality* aspect. If more than a certain amount of fissionable material is accumulated in one container, a nuclear fission chain reaction ensues, as described in Chapter 6; this must be, and easily can be, avoided in chemical manipulations because the consequences can be serious.

Much work on the chemical properties of americium has been carried out with americium-241, which also is difficult to handle since it has a relatively high specific alpha radioactivity, emitting about 7×10^9 alpha particles per minute per milligram. (The tendency of americium and the other transuranium elements to lodge in the bone, however, is not nearly so great as that of plutonium.) The isotope americium-243 has a specific alpha activity some 15 to 20 times less than americium-241 and is thus a more attractive isotope for chemical investigation.

The isotope principally used for early investigations of curium on the macroscopic scale was curium-242 (with a specific disintegration rate of approximately 7×10^{12} alpha particles per minute per milligram). Obviously, such work with curium-242 is extremely difficult, and use of this isotope was discontinued after early work with it. By way of example, the heat produced by the radioactivity would evaporate a dilute (millimolar) solution of curium-242 salts in water to dryness in a short time. Determination of compound structures by X-ray analysis is very difficult when curium-242 is used, because of the very rapid damage to the crystal lattices noted above, and is still somewhat difficult when the longer-lived curium-244 is employed. Curium-244, as it became available, was used more and more for work with weighable quantities. The heavier curium isotopes are less radioactive and offer great advantage in experimental work. Of all the curium isotopes, curium-247 and -248 appear to be potentially the most useful for chemical studies.

Berkelium-249 and californium (first as a mixture of the isotopes californium-249, -250, -251, and -252, and later as californium-249 produced by the decay of berkelium-249) are used in weighable amounts to investigate the macroscopic properties of berkelium and californium. Weighable amounts of berkelium and californium are very difficult to handle, also, because of their intense radioactivity. Spontaneous fission is one mode of decay for californium-252 (half-life, 2.2 years), one microgram of which emits approximately 2×10^8 neutrons per minute. Californium produced in the highest flux reactors unfortunately contains californium-252 and californium-254, and this makes it very difficult to handle because of the difficulty of achieving shielding against neutrons.

In work with more than a few micrograms of californium-252, or with less than microgram amounts of californium-254, it is necessary to do all manipulations by remote control; this is particularly awkward in work on such a small scale. Fortunately, it is possible to obtain californium-249 through the decay of berkelium-249. This californium isotope has a long spontaneous fission half-life; therefore neutron emission is not a problem.

Einsteinium, as the isotope einsteinium-253 (half-life, 20 days), has been isolated in macroscopic quantity. The isotope einsteinium-254 (half-life, 250 days) is more useful for work with macroscopic quantities. The short half-life and the associated intense radioactivity again make experimental studies difficult.

Ion-exchange Techniques

As discussed earlier (Chapters 2 and 3), the discovery and identification of the actinide elements rest upon the fact that they are a family whose heavier members correspond closely in chemical traits to the members of the known, naturally-occurring lanthanide family. This was the key to the discovery of elements 95 and 96 (americium and curium); in addition, the recognition that these elements were members of an actinide transition series was absolutely essential to the discovery of the elements beyond curium through element 102. Because the chemical behavior of the actinides is similar and analogous to the lanthanides, separation of various transuranium elements by ordinary chemical means is extremely difficult. It was therefore fortunate that, concurrent with the early work on the transuranium elements, the ion-exchange technique for chemical separation of inorganic ions was being developed. This technique is selective, rapid, and if necessary, can be used with only a few atoms of an element. The ion-exchange technique was a key to the discovery of the transcurium elements in that the elution order and approximate peak positions for the undiscovered elements were predicted with considerable confidence and accuracy. Thus, the first experimental observation of the chemical behavior of the elements from berkelium through mendelevium has been by means of their ion-exchange behavior, coincident with the discovery in each case.

All of the elements present in the tripositive oxidation state in a mixture of actinides and/or lanthanides can be placed in simple chemical combination with an organic polymer (or resin) of a type that has exchangeable cations. (Ions in the other oxidation states also can undergo this reaction, but the chemical identification experiments have utilized the tripositive ions.) The tripositive actinide or lanthanide ions in aqueous solution undergo a simple chemical exchange (*ion-exchange* reaction) when the solid organic polymer is stirred into the solution. This solid material then may be placed at the top of a glass column filled with more of the organic polymer or resin which does not contain the actinides or lanthanides, as shown in Figure 27. The actinide or lanthanide element can then be dissolved (*eluted*) from the resin by pouring through it an *eluant* solution which usually has in it a substance that forms complex ions with the actinide or lanthanide ions. The whole process of ion exchange thus bears a close resemblance to the well-known chromatography techniques.

The chemical reactions which occur in the case of cation-exchange resins can be depicted as follows:

$$M^{+3}_{(aq)} + 3\,NH_4R_{(s)} \rightleftharpoons MR_{3(s)} + 3\,NH_4^{+}_{(aq)}$$

$$M^{+3}_{(aq)} + 4\,A^{-}_{(aq)} \rightleftharpoons MA_4^{-}_{(aq)}$$

where M^{+3} represents the tripositive actinide or lanthanide ions, the

FIGURE 27. *An ion-exchange apparatus used to separate actinide (and/ or lanthanide) elements.*

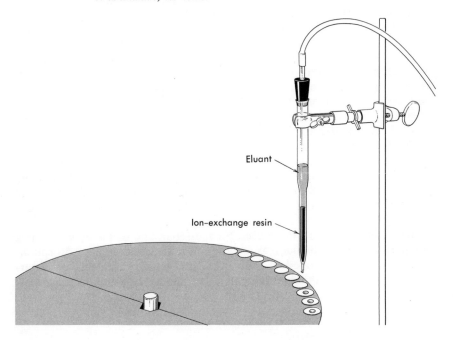

Eluant

Ion-exchange resin

NH_4R represents the ion-exchange resin with the exchangeable cation (NH_4^+) and a polymer residue (R^-) which does not participate in the reaction, the (A^-) represents the anion which forms complex ions with the actinide or lanthanide ions, and (MA_4^-) represents an example of a formula for the complex ion that is formed.

An example of a cation-exchange resin widely used in the separation of the transuranium elements is Dowex-50 resin, a copolymer of styrene and divinylbenzene in which sulfonic acid functional groups have been introduced. Here, the exchangeable cation is H^+, which can be replaced by NH_4^+ or one of the actinide or lanthanide ions, while the polymer residue, R, is the remaining inactive resin structure.

The actinide ions can, in general, be removed from the resin by *elution* with such ions as chloride, nitrate, sulfate, and especially citrate, lactate, alpha-hydroxyisobutyrate, and ethylenediaminetetraacetate. The elution order of adsorbed ions depends on a balance between the degree of adherence to the resin and the strength of the complex ion formed with the eluting agent, and for both the actinide and lanthanide groups of ions, is often in the inverse order of the atomic number.

In certain well-behaved systems, the lanthanide elements are washed (eluted) from the resin in the inverse order of their atomic numbers. That is, lutetium (no. 71) can be collected in the drops coming through the bottom of the column as the first element to emerge, ytterbium (no. 70) as the second element, and so on. The elution data for elements down to europium (no. 63) are shown in Figure 28.

Similarly for the actinides, lawrencium (no. 103) is predicted to leave the column first, to be followed by element 102, and so on down the scale of atomic numbers, as shown in Figure 28. The experimental data for mendelevium (no. 101), fermium (no. 100), and down to americium (no. 95), are shown in Figure 28. The element-by-element analogy between corresponding actinide and lanthanide elements (e.g., americium and europium, curium and gadolinium, berkelium and terbium, etc.) is evident. It was this principle that made it possible to predict the elution positions of the elements from berkelium through mendelevium before their discovery, and which makes it possible, today, to predict the elution positions of element 102 and lawrencium.

The formation of negatively-charged complex ions with anions permits adsorption and elution from anionic exchange resins such as Dowex-1 (copolymer of styrene and divinylbenzene with quaternary ammonium groups) and Amberlite IRA-400 (polystyrene, quaternary amine), and the order of elution is often the reverse of that from the cationic-exchange resins.

Ion-exchange resins can be used for the separation of the actinides as a group from the lanthanides as a group. In the case of the adsorption-elution systems illustrated in Figure 28, the actinide elements are intermingled with the lanthanide elements according to their elution sequences.

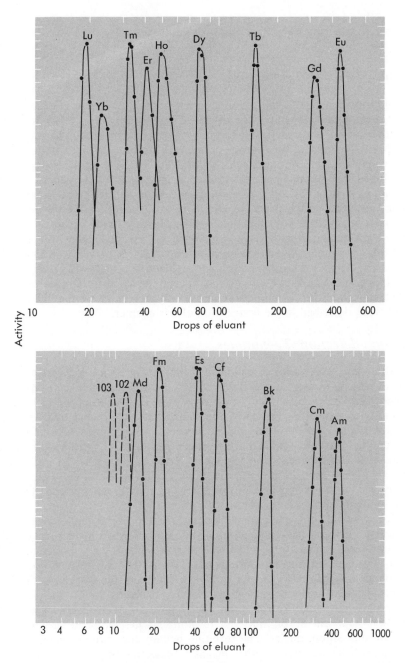

FIGURE 28. *Elution of tripositive lanthanide and actinide ions from Dowex-50 ion-exchange resin with ammonium alpha-hydroxyisobutyrate. The predicted positions for elements 102 and 103 are indicated by dotted lines.*

Special Chemical Techniques

Ultramicrochemical and submicrogram techniques for investigation of the transuranium elements were discussed in Chapter 2 (cf. plutonium and californium). If extremely small volumes are used, by employing capillary tubing as containers, microgram or lesser quantities of material will give relatively high concentrations in solution. Very sensitive balances have been developed that permit quantitative measurements with exceedingly minute quantities of material; some of these balances can be used to measure magnetic forces due to the paramagnetic nature of the ions. Since the amounts of material involved are often too small to be seen with the unaided eye, the actual chemical work is usually done on the mechanical stage of a microscope, where all of the essential apparatus is in view. Compounds prepared on such a small scale can be identified successfully by X-ray crystallographic methods. Often these special chemical techniques must be combined with the techniques required for protection of the laboratory worker, as described in the first section of this chapter.

Radiation-detection Techniques

Although the physical detection of radioactivity is not a chemical technique, its importance in the discovery of the transuranium elements and isotopes and in chemical studies warrants some discussion of the techniques of radiation detection. Basically, the radioactive decay of a transuranium isotope is detected by observing the results of the physical interaction of the emitted particle (alpha particle, beta particle, or neutron), or spontaneous fission fragments, or gamma or X ray, with matter. In each case, there is a local deposition of energy in matter, when one of these emissions is stopped, which excites and ionizes a large number of neighboring atoms— in a sense an amplification effect.

For example, in a gas one alpha particle can excite and ionize many thousands of molecules and atoms. This ionization effect can be readily detected as a result of the electrical current across a gap, which is normally insulated by the un-ionized gas. This is the principle of operation of ionization chambers, Geiger counters, and neutron detectors. (In the latter, the uncharged neutron itself does not directly ionize the detector material, such as boron trifluoride (BF_3) gas; it first undergoes a nuclear reaction with the boron nucleus, resulting in the emission of energetic helium and tritium nuclei. The resulting helium and tritium nuclei are the actual particles detected.) Other means of detecting these excited atoms in solids are by the light these atoms emit upon de-excitation (scintillation counter) or by the changes they produce in a semi-conductor's physical characteristics (solid state detectors).

The emitting radioactive sample to be measured is generally placed as close as possible to the detector to insure a high geometrical efficiency for intercepting and stopping the emissions. Also, the physical effects observed, such as the ionization of a gas or a scintillation in a transparent solid, are still weak signals and must be further amplified, usually by elaborate electronic means to assure that there is no distortion of the data, until the strengthened signal can be counted on a register, photographed on an oscilloscope, or recorded in other ways.

5

Future

Transuranium

Elements

Predicted Stability

The eventual discovery of additional transuranium elements seems to be assured. Studies of the known isotopes of the transuranium elements have already made possible the prediction of the decay properties of new isotopes. Unfortunately the prospects for producing ever higher transuranium elements seem poor, for the predictions suggest proportionately shorter half-lives for these elements as their atomic number increases. (This is shown in Figure 29, which uses data of the type described in Chapter 10.) The approximate nature of the predictions is illustrated by the range of the half-lives shown in Figure 29.

It is difficult to predict the number of additional transuranium elements having isotopes with sufficiently long half-lives to permit chemical identification. It may be noted, however, that any of these nuclides could have a specially hindered decay, leading to longer half-lives than those predicted for average nuclides. The nuclei with odd numbers of protons or neutrons have the longest half-lives (see Chapter 10), and therefore such nuclei offer the best hope for the discovery of the "trans-actinide" elements (i.e., the elements beyond lawrencium, the last element in the actinide series).

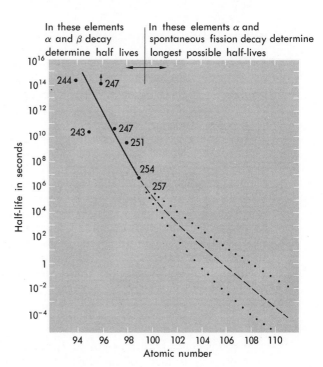

In these elements
α and β decay
determine half lives

In these elements α and
spontaneous fission decay determine
longest possible half-lives

Half-life in seconds

244 •   • 247

243 •   • 247
          • 251

          254

          257

94   96   98   100   102   104   106   108   110

Atomic number

FIGURE 29. *Predicted half-lives (indicated by broken line) of the longest-lived isotopes up to element 110. Mass numbers of known longest-lived isotopes are indicated. These predications are approximate and can serve only as the most general guides; the dotted lines thus indicate the range of predicted half-lives.*

The former basic criterion for the discovery of a new element—namely, chemical identification and separation from all previously-known elements —had to be changed in the case of lawrencium (element 103). This also may be true for elements beyond lawrencium. Thus, even if chemical identification is not possible, careful measurements of decay properties and production yields and mechanisms, and the clever use of recoil techniques, eventually should allow the extension of effective identification to another half-dozen elements or so beyond the heaviest now known. The Berkeley group has continued to work out techniques that should eventually allow exact mass number identification of nuclides with half-lives as short as milliseconds and approximate identification of mass number for those in the microsecond range.

The first isotopes of many of the new elements that will be discovered in the future probably will be identified through the use of such physical methods. The production of isotopes with sufficiently long half-lives to allow chemical identification may follow later. For the isotopes with very short half-lives, some chemical identification probably can be made by using simpler and faster methods involving migration of atoms or ions, volatility, reactions with surfaces, or gas-flow reactions.

There have been a number of suggestions that very heavy elements, and especially an element with atomic number 137 or higher, would undergo a collapse of outer atomic electrons into the nucleus because of the large positive charge of the nucleus. However, J.A. Wheeler has been able to show that for atoms with atomic numbers substantially higher than 137 the atomic or extranuclear electrons would behave normally because of the finite extension of the nucleus. Accordingly, it would appear that there is no limitation on the existence of such heavy elements from the standpoint of the extranuclear electronic structure of such atoms; the limitation comes as a result of nuclear instability.

The production of such ultraheavy nuclei would require extremely large numbers of neutrons flowing through a unit area in a unit time—that is, extremely high neutron fluxes, of the order of 10^{30} neutrons per square centimeter per second, such as may be present in stars. It is difficult to see how such very heavy nuclei can be made on earth. There is no indication that such nuclei can be produced and detected because the rate of decay increases too rapidly as the atomic number increases. Unless unexpected islands of stability due to closed neutron or proton shells are found, predictions based on regularities in decay properties suggest, as stated above, that it should not be possible to produce and detect elements beyond another half-dozen or so.

Predicted Chemical Properties

It is scientifically disappointing, of course, that there is little possibility of producing isotopes of elements with atomic numbers higher than einsteinium having sufficient stability for a full study of their properties other than through the use of the tracer technique. The extended study of the actinides with macroscopic (weighable) quantities has done much to clarify the chemical relationship of elements belonging to an "f" transition series (previously known only in the rare-earths), and it would be very interesting to carry such studies forward to include all of the actinides (see Chapters 8 and 9).

The situation is even more disappointing with respect to the heavier transuranium elements, for if this limit did not exist one might some day hope to produce a wholly new kind of transition series of eighteen "5g" elements. (Here, the "g" designates the next subshell beyond the "f" subshell in the inner 5th major electron shell.) To study the properties of these elements, even through the use of the tracer technique, would be immensely fascinating, but it seems to be impossible because predictions indicate that electrons would not begin to occupy the 5g shell before about atomic number 120.

Rough predictions of the chemical properties of elements beyond mendelevium seem, at least, to be quite straightforward. Lawrencium completes the actinide series, and it is expected that elements 104, 105, 106, etc., will be fitted into the Periodic Table under hafnium, tantalum, tungsten, etc., and these elements can therefore be referred to as ekahafnium, ekatantalum, ekatungsten, etc. The filling of the 6d electronic shell at element 112 should be followed by the addition of electrons to the 7p shell until the rare-gas structure is attained at hypothetical element 118 (see Chapters 3 and 8).

It seems quite certain that the chemical identification of elements 102 and lawrencium eventually will be made, using the ion-exchange technique described in Chapter 4 as well as knowledge of their homologues, ytterbium and lutetium, and other actinide elements. Element 102 might be expected to have a stable tripositive oxidation state and, like its homologue ytterbium, a somewhat unstable dipositive state that may be of importance in the chemical identification of the element. The dipositive state of element 102, if it is comparable in stability to the dipositive state of ytterbium, may permit a rapid separation of element 102 from the other actinide elements by electrolytic or amalgam reduction, with ytterbium as a carrier. The stability of the dipositive state may be reflected in the properties of the metallic state of the element—an unusually low density and a relatively high volatility. Element 103 might be expected to have only a tripositive oxidation state. Element 104 should be exclusively tetrapositive in aqueous solution and should resemble its homologue, hafnium. Element 105 should resemble niobium and tantalum, and to some extent protactinium, with the pentapositive oxidation state expected to be the most important. The chemical properties of element 106 can be predicted from those of tungsten, molybdenum, and to some extent chromium; thus, we might expect to find the III, IV, V, and VI oxidation states. Elements 107, 108, 109, 110, etc., would be expected to have chemical resemblance to rhenium, osmium, iridium, and platinum, respectively.

Methods of Production

The preparation of transfermium elements by the process of multiple neutron capture as a result of intense neutron bombardment over long periods of time (see Figure 32, Chapter 7) requires extremely high neutron fluxes because some of the intermediate isotopes have half-lives so short as to inhibit their growth to the required concentrations. Fortunately, there are two other methods that offer promise for the production of elements of higher atomic number than those now known.

One method consists of a refinement of the thermonuclear explosion ("Mike") which resulted in the discovery of einsteinium and fermium. A specially designed nuclear device and a carefully chosen test site to enhance the production and recovery of these very heavy elements are required to ensure the success of such experiments. The nuclear explosion, to be successful, must be conducted so that a source material such as uranium-238 (or heavier nuclides of higher atomic number) is subjected to an extremely intense flux of neutrons in an extremely short time (a few microseconds). Figure 30 shows nuclides, including some relatively rich in neutrons, that are predicted to be produced by this method. Here, again, the predicted short half-lives of the new transuranium elements that might be synthesized in this manner may make recovery and identification very difficult.

Perhaps the best method for the production of new transuranium elements, producing nuclides deficient in neutrons, is that already used in the discovery of element 102 and lawrencium—namely, bombardment with heavy ions. These ions can be accelerated in conventional cyclotrons or in linear accelerators. A linear accelerator capable of producing substantial beams of all the heavy ions from helium to neon, and smaller, usable beams of ions as heavy as those of argon, has been in operation at the University of California since 1958. A similar accelerator is in operation at Yale University. Scientists in the Soviet Union have shown great interest in heavy ions and their application to the synthesis of transuranium elements, and they now have in operation several heavy-ion accelerators. Heavy-ion accelerators are available for experiments of this type in other laboratories throughout the world as well.

Even with the use of heavy ions, the source of target materials presents serious problems. The Atomic Energy Commission has a program to produce such target materials in significant quantities, as discussed in Chap-

FIGURE 30. *Possible nuclides that might be produced through use of a nuclear explosion as source of neutrons to be absorbed in uranium for production of nuclides of higher atomic number than now known. The predicted short half-lives of elements synthesized in this manner may make recovery and identification very difficult.*

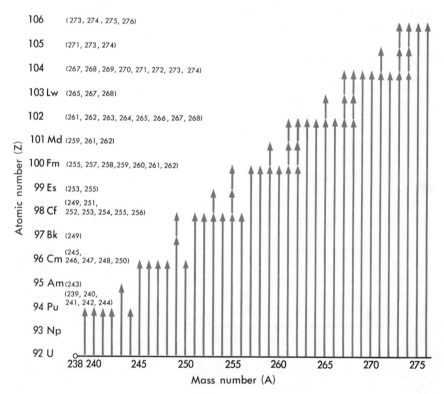

ter 7. Even after procurement of the target material, problems are caused by the heating of the target due to the energy loss of the heavy ion beam passing through it and by other difficulties of handling the large amount of radioactivity in the target.

Also, the yields of the reactions for the production of heavy transuranium elements through the use of heavy ions are extremely small, since so large a proportion of the intermediate compound nuclei produced undergo the fission reaction. The largest yield (i.e., cross section, see Chapter 10) for the production of a very heavy transuranium nuclide through heavy-ion bombardment is obtained by using heavy ions of the smallest possible atomic number. Such ions permit the formation of intermediate compound nuclei which undergo the least fission because they have the least energy of excitation. Thus, a larger cross section for the formation of an isotope of element 106 will result from the bombardment of einsteinium (no. 99) with nitrogen ions (no. 7) than from curium (no. 96) plus neon ions (no. 10).

Element 104 probably will be produced through the bombardment of californium with carbon ions—perhaps even before this book is published or shortly thereafter. This might be followed by the synthesis of element 105 utilizing californium plus nitrogen ions—if this is accomplished before microgram amounts of einsteinium-254 become available. Einsteinium-254, if available, might be bombarded with the lighter carbon ions to produce element 105. The still heavier elements probably will be synthesized through the bombardment of californium or einsteinium with heavy ions of ever-increasing atomic number. As described above, irradiation with neutrons from nuclear explosions will offer an alternative method of producing such elements; such neutrons can be used to irradiate nuclides of ever-increasing atomic number, as these become available.

Hopefully, the experimental difficulties now foreseen for the production of the next group of new transuranium elements will be solved, as they have been in the past, and several more elements will be added to the Periodic Table.

6

Application

of the Transuranium

Elements

The search for and discovery of the transuranium elements was clearly basic research, a quest for further knowledge and understanding of the atomic and nuclear properties of the elements. However, as has often happened in the past, this basic research proved to have practical aspects of outstanding importance to people throughout the world. The most immediate effect that the discovery of a transuranium element had on the world was, of course, with the use of plutonium in the manufacture of nuclear weapons.

During World War II, effort was successfully applied to separating the fissionable uranium isotope, uranium-235, from the bulk of the uranium, uranium-238. An alternative method was vital for producing a fissionable isotope. After the discovery of plutonium-239 and the demonstration of its favorable fissionable properties, an intensive program of research, development, and engineering was sponsored to produce significant quantities of this new element for military uses. The primary nuclear reactions for the production of plutonium in a nuclear reactor, with natural uranium, operating on thermal or slow neutrons (see last section of this chapter for explanation of slow neutrons), are:

(1) $_{92}U^{235} + _{0}n^{1} \longrightarrow$ fission products $+ 2.5_{0}n^{1} +$ energy ($\sim$200 Mev)

(2) $_{92}U^{238} + _{0}n^{1} \longrightarrow {}_{92}U^{239} + \gamma$

$$_{92}U^{239} \xrightarrow[T_{\frac{1}{2}} = 23.5 \text{ m}]{\beta^{-}} {}_{93}Np^{239} \xrightarrow[T_{\frac{1}{2}} = 2.35 \text{ d}]{\beta^{-}} {}_{94}Pu^{239}$$

An integral number of neutrons, say two or three or four, is emitted in each of the dozens of reactions, leading to different pairs of fission products in reaction 1. The number 2.5 represents an over-all average for all of these fission reactions.

One of the neutrons produced in reaction 1 is used to induce the fission reaction in another uranium-235 nucleus (thus continuing a controlled, self-perpetuating nuclear *chain reaction*), while some fraction of the remaining neutrons from reaction 1 are utilized in reaction 2 to produce plutonium-239. In order to produce the required quantities of plutonium-239 in this manner during World War II, two major problems had to be solved—first, the building of nuclear reactors that would operate with natural uranium at a sufficiently high power-level to produce the plutonium at an adequate rate; and, second, the building of a chemical extraction plant in which the plutonium could be separated from the uranium and the highly radioactive fission products, using remote control procedures.

The separation of uranium isotopes required exceedingly refined techniques, since chemically the two isotopes were essentially indistinguishable. The separation of plutonium from the uranium in which it was formed was a more straightforward chemical process. One could rely on the chemical properties of the new element to separate it from uranium and all the other elements present—if one knew the chemical properties of this new element. Fortunately, it was possible—using tracer and ultramicrochemical techniques as described in Chapter 2—to determine the chemical properties of plutonium using tracer and microgram amounts. The engineering of large-scale separation plants based on this knowledge was successful.

The first large site (constructed during World War II) for the production of plutonium was the Hanford Engineer Works at Hanford, Washington. The bismuth phosphate chemical process originally used to separate the irradiated uranium produced by large reactors on the site has been described in Chapter 2. During the intervening years, new chemical separations processes have been developed. The ones most widely used are based on a solvent extraction technique, wherein an organic solvent, immiscible with water, extracts the plutonium and uranium from an aqueous solution. The plutonium is separated from the uranium and further separated from the radioactive fission products by cycling several times between the aqueous solutions and fresh organic solvents, utilizing changes in its oxidation states.

After the war, the production facilities at Hanford were expanded, and a second American plutonium production site—the Savannah River Plant —was constructed on the Savannah River south of Aiken, South Carolina.

Several countries throughout the world have similar facilities for the production of plutonium. Such later production plants are more sophisticated than the one developed during the war, and can have increased efficiency by using uranium fuel slightly enriched in uranium-235 in the production reactors.

Plutonium has important peacetime uses for the production of electric power, as explained in the last section of this chapter. It can also be used to fuel reactors furnishing neutrons for the production of radioactive isotopes, which have a myriad of uses in medicine, agriculture, industry, and science, including many areas of basic and applied research.

The large amounts of energy available in the nuclear-fission reaction, through the propagation by neutrons of a self-sustaining nuclear chain reaction, can be utilized in two general ways. When a neutron of any energy strikes the nucleus of one of the nuclides (plutonium-239, uranium-235, or uranium-233) which is capable of undergoing fission with thermal (essentially zero energy) neutrons, the fission reaction can occur in a self-sustaining manner. The initial fission reaction gives rise to the further release of neutrons, which cause further fission, with the further release of neutrons, and so on, provided a sufficient quantity (a *critical mass*) of the fissionable nuclide is present. The plutonium-239 can be produced as described above, the uranium-235 by separation from natural uranium, and the uranium-233 by the absorption of neutrons in thorium. This large quantity of nuclear fission energy may be released suddenly in a nuclear explosion, or in a slow, controlled manner, in a nuclear power reactor. Due to the importance of these two uses of nuclear energy, some of the principles upon which they are based are described in the following sections of this chapter. Perhaps the solution of the difficulties standing in the way of the proper international control of nuclear weapons can be aided by a more widespread understanding of the scientific principles involved in their operation.

Conditions for a Nuclear Explosion

The first nuclear device fired, at Alamogordo, New Mexico, on July 16, 1945, ushering in the atomic age, was the first successful test of an explosion using plutonium. Such nuclear explosions have important peacetime as well as military uses. The techniques used to produce a *nuclear explosion* (i.e., an essentially instantaneous, self-perpetuating nuclear chain reaction) are very complex. A nuclear explosion must utilize a high energy neutron spectrum (fast neutrons). This results basically from the fact that, to produce an effective explosion the chain reaction must increase as rapidly as possible, utilizing the high energy neutrons produced in the fission reaction. The process by which a neutron is degraded in energy is time-consuming and largely eliminates the possibility of an explosion. (This also explains why power reactors that operate with a slow or thermal neutron spectrum cannot undergo a nuclear explosion, even if the worst accident is imagined. In the case of reactors that operate with higher energy neutrons, a nuclear explosion is also precluded because of the geometrical arrangement of the fissionable material and the rearrangement of this material if an accident occurs.)

The explosive ingredients of fission weapons are limited to plutonium-239, uranium-235, and uranium-233, because these are the only nuclides that are reasonably long-lived, capable of being produced in significant quantities, and also capable of undergoing fission with neutrons of all energies—from essentially zero or thermal to high energies. Other nuclides—as, for example, uranium-238 or thorium-232—can undergo fission with high energy neutrons, but not with those of lower energy. It is not possible to produce a self-sustaining chain reaction with these nuclides, since an insufficient fraction of the neutrons produced in the fission reaction has sufficient energy to induce, and hence perpetuate, the fission reaction in these nuclides.

If the conditions are such that the neutrons are lost at a faster rate than they are formed by fission, the chain reaction is not self-sustaining. The escape of neutrons occurs at the exterior of the plutonium-239 (or uranium-235 or uranium-233) mass undergoing fission, and thus the rate of loss by escape will be determined by the surface area. On the other hand, the fission process, which results in the formation of more neutrons, takes place throughout the whole of the material; the rate of growth of neutron population is therefore dependent upon the mass. If the quantity of plutonium-239 (or uranium-235 or uranium-233) is small, i.e., if the ratio of the surface area to the volume is large, the proportion of neutrons lost by escape to those producing fissions will be so great that the propagation of a nuclear fission chain, and hence the production of an explosion, will not be possible. But as the size of the piece of plutonium-239 (or uranium-235 or uranium-233) is increased and the relative loss of neutrons is thereby decreased, a point is reached at which the chain reaction can become self-sustaining. This is referred to as the "critical mass" of the fissionable material.

Actually, a critical mass depends in a complex manner on several factors, including the shape of the material, its composition, and the presence of impurities which can remove neutrons in nonfission reactions. For example, by surrounding the fissionable material with a suitable neutron reflector, the loss of neutrons by escape can be reduced and the critical mass can thus be decreased.

Because of the presence of stray neutrons in the atmosphere or the possibility of their being generated in various ways, a quantity of plutonium-239 (or uranium-235 or uranium-233) exceeding the critical mass would be likely to melt or possibly explode. It is necessary, therefore, that before detonation a nuclear weapon should contain no single piece of fissionable material that is as large as the critical mass for the given condition. In order to produce an explosion, the material must then be made supercritical, i.e., made to exceed the critical mass, in a time so short as to completely preclude a subexplosive change in the configuration, such as by melting.

Two general methods have been described for bringing about a nuclear explosion—that is to say, for quickly converting a subcritical system into a supercritical one. (For a more complete description of these methods, see *The Effects of Nuclear Weapons,* listed in the Suggested Further Readings at the end of this book.)

In the first procedure, two or more pieces of fissionable material, each less than a critical mass, are brought together very rapidly in the presence of neutrons to form one piece that exceeds the critical mass. This may be achieved in some kind of gun-barrel device, in which a high explosive is used to blow one subcritical piece of fissionable material from the breech end of the gun into another subcritical piece firmly held in the muzzle end.

The second method makes use of the fact that when a subcritical quantity of an appropriate isotope, i.e., plutonium-239 (or uranium-235 or uranium-233), is strongly compressed, it can become critical or supercritical. The reason for this is that compressing the fissionable material—i.e., increasing its density—increases the rate of production of neutrons by fission relative to the rate of loss by escape. That is, the surface area (or neutron escape area) is decreased, while the mass (upon which the rate of propagation of fission depends) remains constant. A self-sustaining chain reaction may then become possible with the same mass that was subcritical in the uncompressed state.

In a fission weapon, the compression may be achieved by encompassing the subcritical material with a shell of chemical high explosives, which is *imploded* by means of a number of external detonators, so that an inwardly-directed "implosion" wave is produced. When this wave reaches the subcritical mass of plutonium-239 (or uranium-235 or uranium-233), it causes the latter to be compressed in the presence of neutrons so that it becomes supercritical and explodes.

Hydrogen isotopes, such as H^2 (deuterium) or H^3 (tritium) can provide explosive energy as the result of *fusion* reactions (e.g., the fusion of two hydrogen isotopes to form a helium isotope)—for example:

$$H^2 + H^2 \longrightarrow He^3 + n \ + 3.2 \text{ Mev}$$

$$H^2 + H^2 \longrightarrow H^3 \ + H^1 + 4 \text{ Mev}$$

$$H^3 + H^2 \longrightarrow He^4 + n \ + 17 \text{ Mev}$$

$$H^3 + H^3 \longrightarrow He^4 + 2n + 11 \text{ Mev}$$

Temperatures of ten to a hundred million degrees are necessary to make nuclear fusion reactions take place. Relatively large amounts of hydrogen and/or lithium can be heated to such temperatures by utilizing the energy and neutrons from the explosion of fissionable material. Lithium provides a source of tritium when it captures a neutron by the reaction

$$_3Li^6 + _0n^1 \longrightarrow _1H^3 + _2He^4 + 4.5 \text{ Mev}$$

Devices making use of these principles are referred to as hydrogen or thermonuclear bombs.

The energy release can be enhanced further by using the high energy neutrons released in the fusion reactions to induce fission in the abundant isotope, uranium-238. Thus, we have fission-fusion and fission-fusion-fission weapons, which can give rise to explosions of much greater energy than those from simple fission weapons. The radioactive "fall-out" from such explosions mainly consists of the fission products; thus, the "cleaner" the explosion, the higher the proportion of fusion to fission reactions. However, neutrons from either type of reaction produce radioactive carbon-14 (as a result of the reaction with nitrogen in the air), induce radioactivity in the device's component materials, and also in the soil and neighboring material, when exploded close to the ground.

Nuclear explosions, besides their military uses, have important peaceful applications to large-scale excavation, to uses where high temperatures and pressures are needed, such as in mining and the recovery of oil from shales, and to numerous research uses, such as the production of isotopes. The American work in this field of applications is known as the *Plowshare* program, a name which is derived from the concept based on Isaiah's prophecy: ". . . and they shall beat their swords into plowshares, and their spears into pruninghooks: nation shall not lift up sword against nation, neither shall they learn war any more."

Production of Nuclear Power

The fissionable nuclides, however, are fortunately not limited to explosive uses only. They also have additional and important peaceful applications. A controlled, self-perpetuating chain reaction, using the nuclides plutonium-239, uranium-235, or uranium-233 as a *nuclear fuel,* can be maintained in such a manner that the energy in the form of heat can be extracted and used either as heat or converted by more or less conventional means to electrical energy. If a critical mass of such fissionable material is present, such a *power reactor* can operate at any power level from essentially zero to thousands of megawatts (a megawatt equals one million watts) with thermal (slow) neutrons, intermediate energy neutrons, or fast (original fission energy) neutrons. The chain reaction is controlled by the proper insertion of neutron-absorbing material, i.e., *control rods,* as is shown in Figure 31 on page 64.

The transuranium nuclides—plutonium-239 and plutonium-241 (produced by the successive absorption of two neutrons by plutonium-239)—which are both fissionable by thermal neutrons, can be used in such power-producing reactors. No large-scale reactors fueled exclusively with plutonium are expected to be in operation before about 1970 (due in large part to the difficulty of handling plutonium because of its alpha-radioactivity); rather, natural uranium or *enriched* uranium (i.e., uranium containing a larger proportion of uranium-235 than the 0.7 per cent present in natural uranium) will continue to be used for some years. Most large reactors using either natural or slightly enriched uranium produce considerable quantities of plutonium, some of which is utilized in the nuclear reaction as it proceeds. The remainder is available upon chemical sep-

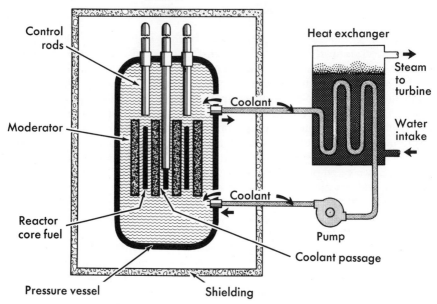

Reactor

Control rods

Heat exchanger

Steam to turbine

Coolant

Moderator

Water intake

Coolant

Reactor core fuel

Pump

Coolant passage

Pressure vessel

Shielding

FIGURE 31. *The location of fuel, moderator, control rods, and coolant, in a typical power reactor. These components are enclosed within a "pressure vessel" containing the various parts of the reactor. The coolant, heated to high temperature by the nuclear fuel, flows through a heat exchanger where it converts water, in a secondary system of pipes, into steam. The steam is then piped to a turbine which operates an electric generator.*

aration of the fuel material. As more reactors come into operation, more plutonium will be produced; and as the problems of handling plutonium are solved, it will become more feasible to use this increasing supply of plutonium for fueling reactors—first, perhaps, by providing a slight plutonium enrichment to natural uranium.

The really important role of plutonium-239 in peaceful applications lies in the fact that it is a fissionable nuclide that can be produced from uranium-238, an isotope that is not readily fissionable. In any analysis of the world's energy resources, it is evident that gas, oil, and coal, are not inexhaustible, but supplies of these are eventually limited. Studies to date indicate that the energy locked in uranium is greater by many powers of ten than that in fossil fuels. This total nuclear energy resource is calculated, however, on the basis of utilization of not only the 0.7 of a per cent of uranium-235 present, but also on the basis of the inherent energy in the 99.3 per cent of uranium-238 that can be converted into plutonium-239. Similarly, thorium-232 represents an equally large energy resource, which can be used by producing the fissionable nuclide, uranium-233 (through the reaction sequence $Th^{232} + n \longrightarrow Th^{233} \longrightarrow Pa^{233} \longrightarrow U^{233}$).

The complete utilization of nonfissionable uranium-238 (through conversion to fissionable plutonium-239) and nonfissionable thorium-232 (through conversion to fissionable uranium-233) can be accomplished through the development of *breeder* reactors. In essence, these reactors produce more fissionable material than they use in the nuclear reaction. This is possible because a fissioning atom of plutonium-239, uranium-235, or uranium-233, emits in excess of two neutrons. In a simplified view, one neutron is required to continue the chain reaction. The remaining neutrons (more than one) theoretically can be captured in uranium-238 or thorium-232 to produce more new fissionable material—plutonium-239 or uranium-233—than is consumed in the process.

In reality, the situation is somewhat more complex. Other parasitic materials present in the reactor capture neutrons. All the fissionable nuclides do not always fission upon capturing neutrons; instead, a certain fraction of the neutrons, dependent upon their energy, is absorbed to produce a heavier isotope (such as plutonium-240 or uranium-234). Development of these theories and studies shows that use of the uranium-238/plutonium-239 breeding cycle is most profitable in a *fast reactor*—that is, a reactor which operates with high energy or fast neutrons. On the other hand, the thorium-232/uranium-233 breeding cycle seems more feasible in a *thermal reactor*—one that uses low energy or thermal neutrons. Breeding of nuclear fuels is an area of reactor research and development in which great advances remain to be made. Over the next decade, this area might make one of the most exciting stories of man's technological development.

Thermal, or slow, neutron reactors require the presence of neutron-slowing materials, i.e., *moderator* material. Because neutrons are slowed most efficiently by collisions with light nuclei that do not have excessive affinities for capturing them, materials like ordinary water, hydrogen-containing organic substances, heavy water, beryllium, and graphite, are favored as moderators. To utilize the heat generated by the fission reaction, all power reactors—including those operating with thermal, intermediate energy, or fast neutrons—require a heat transfer or cooling fluid. Examples of such fluids include ordinary water; heavy water; gases like helium, carbon dioxide, nitrogen, or ordinary air; radiation-resistant organic substances; and liquid metals like lithium, sodium, and potassium. The heat energy in these fluids is usually converted to electrical energy by means of rather conventional turbogenerators, although research on conversion through thermoelectric and thermionic methods is under way. Materials of construction present difficulties, due to the effects of the high levels of radiation and the high temperatures of operation required for efficient conversion of the heat to electrical energy. Complicated chemical processing plants are required for the separation of the neutron-absorbing, radioactive fission product "poisons" and for the recovery of the unused or produced nuclear fuel. Although solvent extraction procedures are generally used, more advanced methods which eliminate the need to dissolve the material are under laboratory investigation; examples of such "dry methods" are pyrometallurgical and volatility procedures.

In areas of the United States and other countries where the cost of the fossil fuels is high, electrical power developed from nuclear fission through simple, nonbreeder reactors is, or soon will be, economically competitive with that developed from conventional fossil fuels, such as coal, oil, and gas. This is initially true for large nuclear power reactors only, i.e., reactors that develop more than three or four hundred megawatts of electrical power. It is only a matter of time, however, before nuclear power will be generally competitive with other methods of electrical power production and will find widespread civilian use, especially through the use of breeder reactors. Many large, first-generation civilian nuclear power reactors are already in operation in many countries of the world.

Nuclear power also finds, or will find, widespread application to marine propulsion—in submarines, other warships, and merchant ships—because of capability for high speed and extremely long range (literally hundreds of thousands of miles before refueling). It finds special application in power stations wherever long-time, unattended operations are required, such as at the North or South Pole or other remote regions. Nuclear reactors can also heat propellants for the propulsion of long-range, large-payload space vehicles. Another special application of light-weight, compact power reactors is to furnish electric power to communication and other satellites and to furnish the large amounts of electrical energy needed for electrical propulsion for extremely long-range, large-payload space vehicles. Nuclear power will not find direct application to automobiles because of the large weight (of the order of 100 tons) of material required for shielding from radiation produced by the nuclear-fission reaction.

The application of the transuranium elements does not end with plutonium-239. One of the more exciting aspects gaining increased importance is the use of certain of these nuclides, such as plutonium-238, curium-242, and curium-244, as concentrated sources of power by themselves. As is discussed in Chapter 10, transuranium elements emit high-energy alpha particles. A few grams of such a nuclide, in an appropriately shielded container, can provide an intense source of heat, since the alpha particles are very easily stopped and their energy converted into heat. Using thermoelectric and thermionic devices without moving parts, it is possible to convert this heat into usable electricity.

Such a package power source is both small and light. Already, many uses have been made of it. The first nuclear energy used in space was in 1961, in the form of radioisotope sources (utilizing plutonium-238) in the *Transit* navigational satellites. It is also possible to utilize curium-242 as a power source in space studies—for example, in studies of the lunar surface. These package radioisotope electric generators also can be used to power communication satellites. In addition to space applications, they can be used for terrestrial sources of energy wherever compact and long-lived sources, not requiring much maintenance, are needed at remote sites. Thus, they will affect our lives in many ways.

Another application of these nuclides is the use of some of them, perhaps californium-252 or -254, as a concentrated neutron source. These heavier isotopes decay in an appreciable part by spontaneous fission and release several neutrons per disintegration. There are many interesting applications for such an intense, concentrated source of neutrons. For example, they would find use wherever the more conventional neutron sources, such as plutonium-beryllium or radium-beryllium, are applied; in such sources, neutrons are produced from the reaction of alpha particles with the beryllium nuclei. Actual uses of neutron sources, at present, range from basic research studies through activation analysis to the mapping of oil wells.

It is quite evident that even further applications will be found for these transuranium elements and the knowledge gained from them. The time and effort that went into their discovery has been more than justified by the results.

PART TWO

7

Source

of the Actinide

Elements

Only the first five members of the actinide group, and actinium itself, have been found to occur in nature (i.e., actinium, thorium, protactinium, uranium, neptunium, and plutonium). Actinium and protactinium are decay products of the naturally-occurring uranium isotope uranium-235, but the concentrations present in uranium minerals are small. The methods involved in obtaining them from the natural source are very difficult and very tedious in contrast to the relative ease with which small amounts of these elements may be synthesized. Thorium and uranium occur widely in the earth's crust in combination with other elements. Uranium also occurs in significant concentrations in the oceans. The extraction of these two elements from their ores has been thoroughly studied and developed because of their importance in applications of nuclear energy. Neptunium and plutonium are present in trace amounts in nature— formed by neutron capture in uranium ores; obtaining these elements from this source is not feasible because the concentrations involved are exceedingly small. Some natural abundances for plutonium are given in Table 3.

There is also evidence that the transuranium elements exist in other stellar systems. The study of astrophysics, particularly the use of the spectroscopic techniques, has advanced to a

Table 3 CONCENTRATION OF PLUTONIUM IN
URANIUM ORES

	U %	$Pu^{239}/U \times 10^{12}$
Canadian pitchblende	13.5	7.1
Belgian Congo pitchblende	38	12
Colorado pitchblende	50	7.7
Brazilian monazite	0.24	8.3
North Carolina monazite	1.64	3.6
Colorado fergusonite	0.25	<4
Colorado carnotite	10	<0.4

point where it is possible to obtain considerable detail regarding the abundances of elements in stellar matter, although the transuranium elements themselves have not been observed directly. In addition, theoretical studies on the mechanisms by which the heavier elements are produced from the lighter elements have been rather successful. Thus, in some respects, new element synthesis on earth is a re-creation of the cosmic processes, past and present, that formed all of the chemical elements.

It is now possible to begin to understand how in a stellar system hydrogen is burned first, leading to helium and then to heavier and heavier elements. It is known that the release of energy from the combining of lighter elements to form heavier ones reaches a point, at iron, where more energy is required than is released. It is theorized that as a large star cools after burning most of the available lighter elements, it undergoes a gravitational contraction. This contraction compresses and heats the core to high temperatures. In essence, the potential energy of gravity is converted into sufficient heat to permit the synthesis of elements beyond iron and up through the transuranium region to continue by massive capture of fast neutrons, etc.

For example, the element technetium (no. 43), probably in the form of the isotope technetium-99, with a half-life of 2.1×10^5 years, has been identified in certain stellar systems. Since the half-life of technetium is short, compared to the age of the stellar system, it is evident that the element is being continuously produced.

Interesting evidence for the possible existence of transuranium elements is found in certain classes of novae whose energy output, after the first flare into brilliance, dies out with a half-life of about 55 days. It is conjectured that such a star, just prior to the nova stage, had contracted and converted gravitational energy to thermal energy. This, in turn, began an intense build-up of the lighter elements into heavier elements through the capture of neutrons, ending with a considerable fraction of the material in the form of the transuranium nuclide californium-254. Californium-254 provides a very strong source of energy, since it undergoes spontaneous fission with a half-life of 61 days or almost the half-life observed in the novae. The first such supernova was observed by the Chinese in the year 1054. This suggests the amusing possibility that californium-254 may have been first observed in the skies long before it was synthesized on earth.

There is frequently a need for values to be assigned for the atomic weights of the actinide elements. In most cases, each of the elements has a number of isotopes, some of which can be obtained in isotopically pure form. Any precise experimental work would require a value for the atomic mass of the isotope or isotopic mixture being used; but where there is a purely formal demand for atomic weights, mass numbers chosen on the basis of half-life and availability customarily have been used. A list of these is provided in Table 4.

Table 4   MASS NUMBER OF LONGEST-LIVED OR MORE
AVAILABLE ISOTOPE FOR EACH OF THE ACTINIDE ELEMENTS

Atomic Number and Symbol	Mass Number	Atomic Number and Symbol	Mass Number
89 (Ac)	227	97 (Bk)	249
90 (Th)	232	98 (Cf)	249
91 (Pa)	231	99 (Es)	254
92 (U)	238	100 (Fm)	253
93 (Np)	237	101 (Md)	256
94 (Pu)	242	102 —	254
95 (Am)	243	103 (Lw)	257
96 (Cm)	248		

To study the macroscopic properties of these actinide elements, it is necessary to have weighable amounts. As discussed in Chapter 4, these amounts can be exceedingly small for the new, man-made elements (as small as a few hundredths of a microgram). The isotopes of the transuranium elements that can be produced in weighable quantities are listed in Table 5.

Table 5   TRANSURANIUM NUCLIDES SUITABLE
FOR INVESTIGATIONS WITH WEIGHABLE QUANTITIES

Element	Isotope	Half Life	Element	Isotope	Half Life
Neptunium	Np^{236}	>5000 y		Cm^{246}	5480 y
	Np^{237}	2.20×10^6 y		Cm^{247}	1.64×10^7 y
Plutonium	Pu^{238}	86.4 y		Cm^{248}	4.7×10^5 y
	Pu^{239}	24,360 y		Cm^{250}	2×10^4 y
	Pu^{240}	6580 y	Berkelium	Bk^{247}	7×10^3 y
	Pu^{241}	13.2 y		Bk^{249}	314 d
	Pu^{242}	3.79×10^5 y	Californium	Cf^{249}	360 y
	Pu^{244}	7.6×10^7 y		Cf^{250}	10.9 y
Americium	Am^{241}	458 y		Cf^{251}	800 y (est.)
	Am^{242}	152 y		Cf^{252}	2.2 y
	Am^{243}	7950 y	Einsteinium	Es^{253}	20 d
Curium	Cm^{242}	162.5 d		Es^{254}	250 d
	Cm^{243}	32 y			
	Cm^{244}	17.6 y			
	Cm^{245}	9320 y			

The synthesis of the actinide elements is discussed in order of increasing atomic number in the following sections.

Actinium

Actinium can be prepared by the neutron irradiation of radium-226:

$$_{88}Ra^{226} + {_0}n^1 \longrightarrow {_{88}}Ra^{227}$$

$$_{88}Ra^{227} \xrightarrow[\enspace T_{1/2} = 41.2 \text{ m} \enspace]{\beta^-} {_{89}}Ac^{227} \ (T_{1/2} = 21.7 \text{ y})$$

The actinium is isolated by means of solvent extraction or ion-exchange techniques. In addition, actinium-227, produced in the decay of protactinium-231, can be separated from uranium ore residues.

Protactinium

Similarly, protactinium can be produced by neutron irradiations of thorium-230 (ionium, available from uranium ores):

$$_{90}Th^{230} + {_0}n^1 \longrightarrow {_{90}}Th^{231}$$

$$_{90}Th^{231} \xrightarrow[\enspace T_{1/2} = 25.6 \text{ h} \enspace]{\beta^-} {_{91}}Pa^{231} \ (T_{1/2} = 3.4 \times 10^4 \text{ y})$$

In addition, protactinium-231, produced in the decay of uranium-235, can be separated from uranium ore residues. The methods for the recovery of protactinium include coprecipitation, solvent extraction, ion exchange, and volatility procedures. The recovery is made difficult by the extreme tendency of protactinium (V) to form polymeric ionic species and then colloidal particles. Protactinium in this form is not extractable from water by organic solvents; it tends to adsorb to the surface of containers and may be adsorbed and carried on any precipitates present.

Neptunium

Considerable amounts of neptunium-237 are formed as a by-product of the large-scale synthesis of plutonium in nuclear reactors which use uranium-235 and uranium-238 as fuel. The following nuclear reactions occur, with the relative importance depending on the type of the reactor involved:

$$_{92}U^{238} + {_0}n^1 \longrightarrow {_{92}}U^{237} + 2{_0}n^1$$

$$_{92}U^{237} \xrightarrow[\enspace T_{1/2} = 6.8 \text{ d} \enspace]{\beta^-} {_{93}}Np^{237} \ (T_{1/2} = 2.2 \times 10^6 \text{ y})$$

and

$$_{92}U^{235} + {}_0n^1 \longrightarrow {}_{92}U^{236}$$

$$_{92}U^{236} + {}_0n^1 \longrightarrow {}_{92}U^{237} \qquad {}_{92}U^{237} \xrightarrow[\text{T}_{1/2} = 6.8 \text{ d}]{\beta^-} {}_{93}Np^{237}$$

Historically, the wastes from uranium and plutonium processing of the reactor fuel have been the source of such neptunium. A number of the plutonium chemical processing plants have procedures for routinely recovering such neptunium in the process of recovering the plutonium from the irradiated uranium. Precipitation, solvent extraction, ion exchange, and volatility procedures, can be used to isolate and purify the neptunium. There do not seem to be any practical methods, at least at present, for synthesizing neptunium-236 (half-life, greater than 5000 years) in weighable quantity, because it is not produced by neutron irradiation reactions but only as the result of bombardment with charged particles.

Plutonium

Plutonium as the important isotope plutonium-239 is prepared in multikilogram amounts in nuclear reactors, as described in Chapter 6. In the chain reaction taking place in the reactor, the excess neutrons produced by the fission of uranium-235 are captured in uranium-238 to yield plutonium-239, as follows:

$$_{92}U^{235} + {}_0n^1 \longrightarrow \text{fission products} + 2.5\,{}_0n^1 + \text{energy} (\sim 200 \text{ Mev})$$

$$_{92}U^{238} + {}_0n^1 \longrightarrow {}_{92}U^{239} \xrightarrow[\text{T}_{1/2} = 23.5 \text{ m}]{\beta^-}$$

$$_{93}Np^{239} \xrightarrow[\text{T}_{1/2} = 2.35 \text{ d}]{\beta^-} {}_{94}Pu^{239} \,(\text{T}_{1/2} = 24{,}360 \text{ y})$$

Such plutonium also contains plutonium-240, plutonium-241, and plutonium-242, produced by successive capture of neutrons, in proportions determined by the neutron flux and the length of time the uranium (and therefore the plutonium) is in the reactor. A variety of industrial-scale processes have been developed for the recovery, separation, and purification of plutonium. These can be divided, in general, into the categories of precipitation, solvent extraction, and ion exchange.

The production of plutonium containing a high proportion of plutonium-242, which is more suitable than the lighter isotopes for the chemical investigation of the element, is described in the section below on curium and heavier elements.

The isotope plutonium-238, produced by the reactions:

$$_{93}Np^{237} + {}_0n^1 \longrightarrow {}_{93}Np^{238}$$

$$_{93}Np^{238} \xrightarrow[\mathrm{T}_{1/2} = 2.1\ \mathrm{d}]{\beta^-} {}_{94}Pu^{238}\ (\mathrm{T}_{1/2} = 86.4\ \mathrm{y})$$

is an important fuel for isotopically-powered energy sources used for terrestrial and space satellite applications (as mentioned in Chapter 6). It is produced by irradiating neptunium-237 (produced as described above, in the section on neptunium) with neutrons in nuclear reactors.

Americium

Quantities of americium as americium-241 can be obtained by processing reactor-produced plutonium, which material contains an appreciable proportion of plutonium-241, the parent of americium-241. Separation of the americium is effected by precipitation, ion exchange, or solvent extraction. The longer-lived americium-243 is produced by neutron irradiation, as described in the following section.

Curium, Berkelium, Californium, Einsteinium, and Fermium

The nuclear reaction sequences of neutron captures and beta decays involved in the preparation of the elements with atomic numbers 94 through 100 by means of the slow neutron irradiation of plutonium are indicated in Figure 32. The irradiations are performed by placing the parent material in the core of a high-neutron flux reactor where neutron fluxes in excess of 10^{14} or 10^{15} neutrons per square centimeter per second may be available.

The irradiation of plutonium-239 with neutrons in the Materials Testing

FIGURE 32. *Nuclear reactions for the production of heavy elements by intense slow neutron irradiation. Neutron capture reactions are interspersed with beta decays. Each neutron capture adds one unit to the mass number (horizontal arrows), and each beta decay increases the atomic number by one unit leaving the mass number unchanged (vertical arrows).*

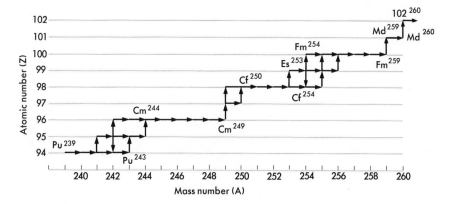

Reactor (MTR) in Idaho (with a neutron flux of 3×10^{14} neutrons per sq. cm. per second), has led to the production of gram quantities of americium (americium-243) and curium (largely curium-244), of multimicrogram quantities of berkelium (berkelium-249) and californium (mass numbers 249, 250, 251, and 252), and of submicrogram quantities of einsteinium (einsteinium-253).

The nuclide curium-242, useful in many applications (see Chapter 6), is produced by neutron irradiation of americium-241, producing americium-242 which undergoes beta decay.

Figure 33 gives, for illustrative purposes, an indication of the time required for the preparation of californium-252 from the starting material, plutonium-242, under conditions of higher neutron fluxes. The yields of the heavier nuclides are reduced as a result of the occurrence of the fission reaction in a number of the nuclides. For example, beginning with 100 grams of plutonium-242, about ten milligrams of californium-252 (together with other isotopes of californium) would be present after two years of continuous irradiation at a neutron flux of 1×10^{15} neutrons per square centimeter per second. Such californium, unfortunately, contains californium-254 (61 days half-life), which is very difficult to handle because of neutron emission in connection with its decay by the spontaneous fission process.

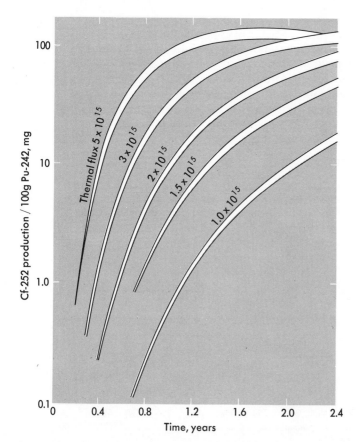

FIGURE 33. *Milligrams of californium-252, produced in neutron irradiations per 100 grams of plutonium-242, as a function of neutron flux (neutrons/sq. cm. / sec.) and time of irradiation.*

A program of the U.S. Atomic Energy Commission is aimed at the production of gram quantities of berkelium-249 and the californium isotopes, and milligram quantities of einsteinium (einsteinium-254) and fermium (fermium-255), through a series of neutron irradiations starting with plutonium-239. This also makes available large quantities of heavy plutonium isotopes, americium-243, and isotopes of curium (a mixture of curium-244 through curium-248, inclusive, with higher proportions of the heavier isotopes resulting from increasing time of neutron irradiation). In the summary table in the Appendix such production reactions are described by the notation "Pu^{239} multiple neutron capture." The nuclides produced are, in general, those with mass numbers above 239, listed in Table 5. The nature of the irradiations and decay chains is such, however, that the plutonium contains very little plutonium-244, the americium very little americium-241 and americium-242, the curium very little curium-242 and curium-243, and the berkelium no berkelium-247.

A number of interesting single isotopes can be made available in macroscopic quantities through this program—for example, pure californium-249 from the beta decay of berkelium-249, and relatively pure curium-248 from the alpha decay of californium-252. It will also be possible to obtain quite pure californium-250, either from the alpha decay of einsteinium-254 or through the short-term neutron irradiation of berkelium-249 (so that the heavier californium isotopes are not built up in quantity).

As shown in Figure 34, in the Atomic Energy Commission program, plutonium-239 (in kilogram amounts) is inserted into a large production reactor; and in several years, this irradiation produces relatively large quantities (hundreds of grams) of plutonium-242, americium-243, and curium-244 (mixed with heavier isotopes and fission products), which, after separation from the fission products, can be used as feed material for further irradiations in the High Flux Isotope Reactor (HFIR) at the Oak Ridge National Laboratory. This reactor, with a neutron flux of 3×10^{15}/neutrons/cm^2/sec, is capable of producing significant quantities of the very heavy elements, as is shown in Figure 33. The products are then separated from the fission products and isolated in the Transuranium Processing Facility (TPF) at Oak Ridge. This is a formidable task, due to the great intensity of radioactivity of the fission products and the heavy transuranium nuclides; the neutron emission from some of the heavy nuclides introduces great difficulties in shielding the operators of the chemical processing plant.

The general transplutonium production program is schematically illustrated in Figure 35. This program is representative of the size of the investment in a reactor, the associated facilities for handling and processing the irradiated transuranium elements, and the actual starting material which is now necessary for further extensive study of the transuranium elements.

Eventually, long irradiations at very high neutron fluxes should produce plutonium-244 and curium with a very high content of curium-248, which will be very useful in the chemical investigation of plutonium and curium. Curium-247 is even better for the investigation of curium, but it will be difficult to produce curium in which this is the main component isotope.

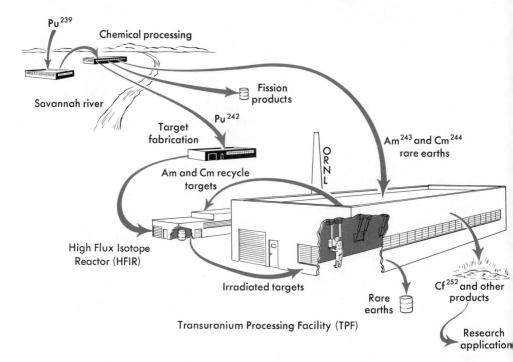

FIGURE 34. *The Atomic Energy Commission's Transplutonium Production Program.*

FIGURE 35. *Program for the production of transplutonium elements.*

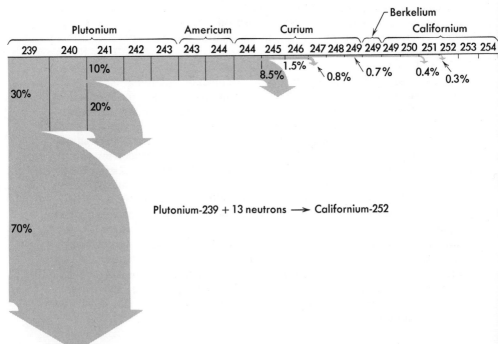

Unfortunately, there does not seem to be any practical method, at least at present, for synthesizing berkelium-247, whose 7000-year half-life would make it ideal for work with weighable quantities of berkelium. This isotope is not produced by neutron irradiation, and it is available only in the small yields that result from bombardment of targets with charged particles.

Mendelevium and Beyond

Neutron irradiation in high-flux reactors cannot be used to prepare the elements beyond fermium (except at extremely high neutron fluxes which are presently unavailable) because some of the intermediate isotopes, which must capture neutrons, have half-lives so short as to preclude their presence in sufficient concentrations.

It is possible to produce very heavy elements in thermonuclear explosions, owing to the very intense, although brief (in the order of a microsecond) neutron flux furnished by the explosion, as discussed in Chapter 5 (see Figure 30). Einsteinium and fermium were first produced in this way, as mentioned in Chapter 2. They were discovered in the fall-out materials from the first thermonuclear explosion (the "Mike" shot) staged in the Pacific in November of 1952. It is possible that elements with atomic numbers greater than 100 would have been found had the debris been examined very soon after the explosion.

The production process involved is multiple neutron capture in the uranium (or other heavy elements) in the device, which is followed by a sequence of beta decays. For example, the synthesis of fermium-255 in the "Mike" explosion was through the production of uranium-255 from uranium-238, followed by a long chain of short-lived beta decays,

$$_{92}U^{255} \xrightarrow{\beta^-} {}_{93}Np^{255} \xrightarrow{\beta^-} {}_{94}Pu^{255} \xrightarrow{\beta^-} \cdots {}_{100}Fm^{255}$$

—all of which occur after the neutron capture reactions are completed. The time-scale in which the addition of these neutrons occurs is so extremely short that the short-lived intermediate products, which otherwise effectively limit the long-term reactor irradiation program, have no effect.

The experimental use of special nuclear devices, exploded underground, can enhance the production and recovery of these very heavy elements. Initial, instantaneous samples of the debris might contain new elements, as well as new isotopes of already-known elements. In addition, after the radioactivity has subsided somewhat, the underground area—still containing valuable, longer-lived transuranium isotopes—can be "mined." It is quite possible, because of their excess of neutrons, that heavy isotopes of known elements like lawrencium and of new elements that might be produced by this method will be longer-lived than the neutron-deficient nuclides produced in bombardments with heavy ions, which of course would offer a substantial advantage in the investigations.

The elements beyond fermium have been prepared in charged-particle bombardments, but in such syntheses the limited availability of heavy elements for target materials, the small reaction yields, and the difficulties in the isolation of very short-lived substances, present very serious problems. It has been possible to make nonchemical separations of short-lived isotopes from the target materials during these bombardments.

Isotopes of mendelevium can be produced by the helium-ion bombardment of einsteinium isotopes:

$$_{99}Es^{253} + {}_2He^4 \longrightarrow {}_{101}Md^{256} \ (T_{1/2} \sim 1\frac{1}{2} \ h) + {}_0n^1$$

$$_{99}Es^{253} + {}_2He^4 \longrightarrow {}_{101}Md^{255} \ (T_{1/2} \sim \frac{1}{2} \ hr) + 2{}_0n^1$$

In both bombardments, the mendelevium isotopes have been isolated from the target material by collecting on a gold foil the atoms of mendelevium which recoil owing to the momentum of the beam of helium ions. When mendelevium was first prepared, only a few atoms of the element were produced, but these were chemically separated successfully and were characterized as having the atomic number 101, as discussed in Chapter 2. A fairly elaborate adaptation of this recoil method has been used in the discoveries of elements 102 and lawrencium.

In order to synthesize the elements beyond mendelevium, it has been necessary to bombard with heavy ions. The syntheses of element 102 through the bombardment of curium with accelerated carbon nuclei, and of lawrencium through the bombardment of californium with accelerated boron nuclei, are described in Chapter 2. The possible synthesis of still heavier elements is discussed in Chapter 5.

The machines used to produce the intense beams of heavy ions used in these bombardments are of two types—cyclotrons and linear accelerators. Cyclotrons of the conventional type can be used to accelerate heavy ions. However, linear accelerators designed for this express purpose are in operation in several laboratories throughout the world. The Heavy Ion Linear Accelerator (HILAC) at Berkeley, with which element 102 and lawrencium first were synthesized, is an example of such a machine.

8

Electronic Structure

of the Actinide

Elements

Intensive study of the heaviest elements has demonstrated that a series of elements similar to the lanthanide series begins at actinium, as discussed in Chapter 3; in this chapter, we will discuss the electronic structure of these actinide elements and their compounds. As this is a somewhat complicated subject, the reader may not have the background necessary to understand the discussion completely; nevertheless, it is felt that such a discussion will be of interest and an incentive to further study.

The electronic configurations of atoms are described by assigning to each extranuclear electron in the atom a quantum designation in terms of a number and a small letter. In this designation of the electron configuration, the *principal quantum numbers* 1, 2, 3, 4, 5, 6, and 7, represent the 1st, 2nd, 3rd, 4th, 5th, 6th, and 7th, major electron shells; and the small letters s, p, d, f, g, represent the subshells (*orbitals*) within each major shell. The 1st major shell has only s electrons, the 2nd major shell can have s and p electrons, the 3rd can have s, p, and d electrons, etc. The number of electrons with identical values for both of these designations is indicated by superscripts. For example, hydrogen has the electronic structure 1s, helium has $1s^2$, lithium has $1s^2 2s$, neon has $1s^2 2s^2 2p^6$, sodium has $1s^2 2s^2 2p^6 3s$, etc.

As the successive elements are built up by adding protons to the nucleus, the successive, added electrons enter the *orbitals* (the spatial description of the motion of an electron) where they have the minimum potential energy, i.e., where they are bound with the most energy. Thus, electrons are sometimes added to outer orbitals before innner orbitals are filled. When these unoccupied orbitals are filled in later elements, as the elements continue to be built up, the so-called transition elements are constituted. For example, in the first (sometimes called iron) group of transition elements, electrons are added to a 3d orbital after the 4s orbital has been filled. The rare-earth, or lanthanide, series of elements is an example of an "inner transition" series. In building up these elements, the inner 4f orbital is being filled in successive lanthanide elements after the filling of the 5s, 5p, and 6s, orbitals in elements of lower atomic number.

The second rare-earth, or actinide, series of elements is another example of an "inner transition" group of elements, where the inner 5f shell is filled in the presence of 6s, 6p, and 7s, electrons. In this case, electrons also enter the 6d orbitals in the early part of the series, because the 5f and 6d electrons have comparable energies. The somewhat loose binding of these electrons accounts for the fact that the early actinide elements are more readily oxidized above the tripositive oxidation state than are the lanthanide elements. Later in the actinide series, the 5f electrons are true inner electrons, as is the case for the 4f electrons throughout most of the lanthanide series, and therefore the chemical properties are not much affected by the successive addition of the shielded f electrons. As a result, these successive elements have nearly identical chemical properties.

Table 6 presents the electronic configuration, or the best prediction for the electronic configuration, of the gaseous atoms of the actinide elements. Similar information for the lanthanide elements is given for purposes of comparison. The configurations enclosed in parentheses are predicted ones.

As shown in Table 6, fourteen 4f electrons are added in the lanthanide series, beginning with cerium (atomic number 58) and ending with lutetium (atomic number 71); and in the actinide elements fourteen 5f electrons are added, beginning formally (though not actually) with thorium (atomic number 90) and ending with lawrencium (atomic number 103). In the cases of actinium, thorium, uranium, and americium, the configurations were determined from an analysis of spectroscopic data obtained by the measurement of the emission lines from neutral and charged gaseous atoms. The knowledge of the electronic structures for protactinium, neptunium, plutonium, and curium, results from atomic-beam experiments.

It is important to realize that the electronic structures listed in Table 6 are those of the neutral (un-ionized) gaseous atoms, whereas it is the electronic structure of the ions and compounds that we are chiefly concerned with in chemistry. The relationship of the electronic structure of the gaseous atom of an element to that of its compounds can be rather complicated. For example, in the case of the actinide and lanthanide elements, one would not necessarily predict the predominance of the III oxidation state from the electronic structures of the gaseous atoms; there are usually

Table 6   ELECTRONIC CONFIGURATIONS FOR GASEOUS ATOMS OF ACTINIDE AND LANTHANIDE ELEMENTS

Atomic Number	Element	Electronic Configuration [a]	Atomic Number	Element	Electronic Configuration [b]
89	actinium	$6d7s^2$	57	lanthanium	$5d6s^2$
90	thorium	$6d^27s^2$	58	cerium	$4f5d6s^2$
91	protactinium	$5f^26d7s^2$	59	praseodymium	$4f^36s^2$
92	uranium	$5f^36d7s^2$	60	neodymium	$4f^46s^2$
93	neptunium	$5f^46d7s^2$	61	promethium	$4f^56s^2$
94	plutonium	$5f^67s^2$	62	samarium	$4f^66s^2$
95	americium	$5f^77s^2$	63	europium	$4f^76s^2$
96	curium	$5f^76d7s^2$	64	gadolinium	$4f^75d6s^2$
97	berkelium	$(5f^86d7s^2$ or $5f^97s^2)$	65	terbium	$4f^96s^2$
98	californium	$(5f^{10}7s^2)$	66	dysprosium	$4f^{10}6s^2$
99	einsteinium	$(5f^{11}7s^2)$	67	holmium	$4f^{11}6s^2$
100	fermium	$(5f^{12}7s^2)$	68	erbium	$4f^{12}6s^2$
101	mendelevium	$(5f^{13}7s^2)$	69	thulium	$4f^{13}6s^2$
102	—	$(5f^{14}7s^2)$	70	ytterbium	$4f^{14}6s^2$
103	lawrencium	$(5f^{14}6d7s^2)$	71	lutetium	$4f^{14}5d6s^2$

Predicted configurations are in parentheses.

[a] In addition to the electronic structure of radon (element number 86), whose electronic configuration is: $1s^2\ 2s^2\ 2p^6\ 3s^2\ 3p^6\ 3d^{10}\ 4s^2\ 4p^6\ 4d^{10}\ 4f^{14}\ 5s^2\ 5p^6\ 5d^{10}\ 6s^2\ 6p^6$

[b] In addition to the electronic structure of xenon (element number 54), whose electronic configuration is: $1s^2\ 2s^2\ 2p^6\ 3s^2\ 3p^6\ 3d^{10}\ 4s^2\ 4p^6\ 4d^{10}\ 5s^2\ 5p^6$

only two so-called "valence electrons," the 7s or 6s electrons, which might indicate a preference for the II oxidation state.

Apparently, specific factors in the crystal structure of, and the aquation (hydration) energies of, the compounds and ions are important in determining the stability of the III oxidation state. Thus, the characteristic tripositive oxidation state of the lanthanide elements is not related directly to the number of "valence electrons" outside the 4f subshell, but is the somewhat accidental result of a nearly constant small difference between large energy terms (ionization potentials on the one hand, and hydration and crystal energies on the other) which persists over an interval of fourteen atomic numbers. Therefore, if we could somehow have a very extended Periodic Table of Elements containing numerous "f" transition series, we might expect that the 5f, rather than the 4f, elements would be regarded as more nearly representative of such f series.

Nevertheless, the electronic structures given in Table 6 will have some relevance to the electronic structures of the ions and compounds of these elements. Fortunately, it is possible to determine the electronic structure of the ions and compounds by a number of methods, such as the measurement of such properties as paramagnetic resonance, paramagnetic susceptibility, light absorption, etc. These measurements, together with consideration of the chemical and other properties of these elements, have provided a great deal of information about the electronic configurations of the aque-

ELECTRONIC STRUCTURE OF THE ACTINIDE ELEMENTS

ous actinide ions and of the actinide compounds. It is interesting to note that these data do show that, in general, all of the electrons—in addition to the radon core—in the actinide compounds and in aqueous actinide ions are indeed in 5f orbitals. There are very few exceptions (such as U_2S_3) and subnormal compounds (such as Th_2S_3) where 6d electrons are present.

Except for the early actinide elements, the III oxidation state is the characteristic oxidation state for each series of elements. As mentioned above, ease of oxidation of the early members of the actinide series is due to the looser binding of the 5f electrons early in the series and the nearness in energy of several electronic levels in this region (7s, 6d, and 5f).

The electronic configurations $5f^7$ or $4f^7$, representing the half-filled f shells of curium and gadolinium, have special stability. Thus, tripositive curium and gadolinium, are especially stable. A consequence of this is that the next element in each case readily loses an extra electron through oxidation, so as to obtain the f^7 structure, with the result that terbium and especially berkelium can be readily oxidized from the III to the IV oxidation state. Another manifestation of this is that europium (and to a lesser extent samarium)—just before gadolinium—tends to favor the $4f^7$ structure with a more stable than usual II oxidation state. Similarly, the stable f^{14} electronic configuration leads to a more stable than usual II oxidation state in ytterbium (and to a lesser extent in thulium) just before lutetium (whose tripositive ion has the $4f^{14}$ structure). This leads to the prediction that element 102, the next to the last actinide element, will have an observable II oxidation state.

After the completion of the 5f shell at lawrencium (element 103), the last actinide element, it is predicted that electrons will be added to the 6d shell in the succeeding transactinide elements. It might be added, mainly for the sake of completeness, that the filling of the 6d shell should be followed by the addition of electrons to the 7p shell, with the attainment of the rare-gas structure at hypothetical element 118. The filling of the 5g shell, corresponding to a wholly new kind of inner transition series of eighteen elements, is predicted to begin at about this region of atomic numbers. It is unfortunate that nuclear instability precludes the possibility of synthesizing and studying such very interesting elements. The predicted electronic structures of some transactinide elements are given in Table 7.

Table 7   PREDICTED ELECTRONIC STRUCTURES
OF SOME TRANSACTINIDE ELEMENTS

Element	Electronic Structure [a]	Element	Electronic Structure [a]
104	$5f^{14}6d^27s^2$	112	$5f^{14}6d^{10}7s^2$
105	$5f^{14}6d^37s^2$	113	$5f^{14}6d^{10}7s^27p^1$
106	$5f^{14}6d^47s^2$	118	$5f^{14}6d^{10}7s^27p^6$
107	$5f^{14}6d^57s^2$	120	$5f^{14}6d^{10}7s^27p^68s^2$
108	$5f^{14}6d^67s^2$	125	$5f^{14}5g^56d^{10}7s^27p^68s^2$

[a] In addition to the electronic structure of randon (element number 86).

9

Chemical and Physical

Properties

of the Actinide

Elements

The chemical resemblance between the actinide elements permits their chemistry to be described for the most part in a correlative way. Therefore, we take up the following in this chapter: oxidation states, hydrolysis, complexion formation, metallic state, solid compounds, crystal structure, and absorption and fluorescence spectra of the actinide elements or compounds.

The similarity in their electronic structures (as discussed in Chapter 8) confers similarity in chemical properties between the actinide and lanthanide elements. The analogy in chemical properties between these two series of elements is of particular importance in the ion-exchange method of separation and identification of the actinide elements and has played an important role in their discovery, as described in Chapters 2 and 4. There is great similarity in the types of chemical compounds formed by the members of the two groups of elements. For example, the tripositive oxidation state occurs widely in each group. The two groups of elements, however, are not entirely comparable in this respect. The tripositive oxidation state characteristic of lanthanide elements does not appear in aqueous solutions of thorium and protactinium and does not become the predominantly stable oxidation state in aqueous solution of the actinides until americium is reached. The elements uranium through americium have several oxidation states, and there is no analogous example among the lanthanide elements. These differences can readily be interpreted as a result of the nearness in the energies of several electronic levels in this region (7s, 6d, and 5f), as discussed in Chapter 8.

Oxidation States

The oxidation states of the actinide elements are summarized in Table 8; the most stable states appear with underlines. The existence of the tripositive oxidation state of thorium, indicated in parentheses, is subject to some doubt.

Table 8 THE OXIDATION STATES OF THE ACTINIDE ELEMENTS

Element Atomic Number	Ac 89	Th 90	Pa 91	U 92	Np 93	Pu 94	Am 95	Cm 96	Bk 97	Cf 98	Es 99	Fm 100
Oxidation states	3	(3)		3	3	3	$\underline{3}$	$\underline{3}$	$\underline{3}$	$\underline{3}$	$\underline{3}$	$\underline{3}$
		$\underline{4}$	4	4	4	4	$\underline{4}$	4	4			
			5	5	5	$\underline{5}$	5					
				6	$\underline{6}$	6	6					

The actinide elements exhibit the uniformity in ionic types attributable to a "rare-earth"-like series. In acid aqueous solution, there are four common types of cations, and these together with their colors are listed in Table 9.

Table 9 ION TYPES AND COLORS FOR ACTINIDE IONS
IN AQUEOUS SOLUTION *

Element	M^{3+}	M^{4+}	MO_2^+	MO_2^{2+}
actinium	colorless	—	—	—
thorium	—	colorless	—	—
protactinium	—	colorless	(colorless)	—
uranium	red	green	(color unknown)	yellow
neptunium	blue to purple	yellow-green	green	pink to red
plutonium	blue to violet	tan to orange-brown	(reddish purple)	yellow to pink-orange
americium	pink	rose	yellow	rum-colored
curium	colorless	unknown	—	—

* M represents an actinide element in general.

The wide variety of colors exhibited by actinide ions is again characteristic of a transition series of elements and is also observed, for example, in the iron-nickel-cobalt and lanthanide transition series of elements. The open spaces indicate that the corresponding oxidation states do not exist in aqueous solution. The color of plutonium (V) has not been observed, since it cannot be prepared free of other oxidation states, but is deduced from the absorption spectrum of its aqueous solution. Protactinium (V) usually exists in aqueous solution as a highly polymerized colloid, and it seems unlikely that $PaO_2{}^+$ as a simple ion is present in such solutions. There is no conclusive evidence for the existence of protactinium (III) either in the solid state or in aqueous solution.

Corresponding ionic types for the actinides are similar in chemical behavior, although the oxidation-reduction relationships, and therefore the relative stabilities, differ from element to element. In the oxidation states V and VI, the actinide ions exist in the forms $MO_2{}^+$ and $MO_2{}^{2+}$ (where again M is used to represent an actinide element in general) which are stable with respect to their binding of oxygen atoms and remain unchanged through a great variety of chemical treatment.

The standard oxidation potentials for the actinide elements are as follows:

Acid aqueous solution:

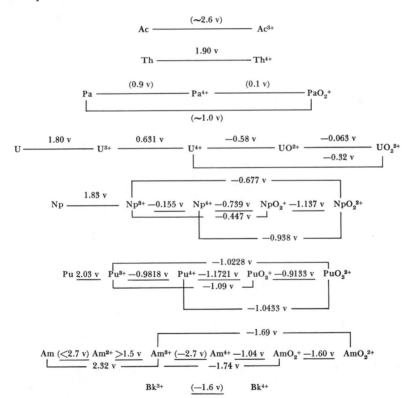

Alkaline aqueous solution:

$$\text{Th } \underline{2.48 \text{ v}} \quad \text{Th(OH)}_4$$

$$\text{U } \underline{2.17 \text{ v}} \quad \text{U(OH)}_3 \; \underline{2.14 \text{ v}} \quad \text{U(OH)}_4 \; \underline{0.62 \text{ v}} \quad \text{UO}_2\text{(OH)}_2$$

$$\text{Np } \underline{2.25 \text{ v}} \quad \text{Np(OH)}_3 \; \underline{1.76 \text{ v}} \quad \text{Np(OH)}_4 \; \underline{-0.39 \text{ v}} \quad \text{NpO}_2\text{OH} \; \underline{-0.48 \text{ v}} \quad \text{NpO}_2\text{(OH)}_2$$

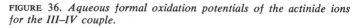
(−0.43 v)

$$\text{Pu } \underline{(2.42 \text{ v})} \quad \text{Pu(OH)}_3 \!\cdot\! \text{x H}_2\text{O} \; \underline{0.95 \text{ v}} \quad \text{Pu(OH)}_4 \!\cdot\! \text{y H}_2\text{O} \; \underline{-0.76 \text{ v}} \quad \text{PuO}_2\text{(OH)}_{aq} \; \underline{-0.26 \text{ v}} \quad \text{PuO}_2\text{ (OH)}_{3^-\text{aq}}$$

∼−0.5 v

$$\text{Am } \underline{2.71 \text{ v}} \quad \text{Am(OH)}_3 \; \underline{-0.4 \text{ to } -0.5 \text{ v}} \quad \text{Am(OH)}_4 \; \underline{(-0.7 \text{ v})} \quad \text{AmO}_2\text{OH} \; \underline{(-1.1 \text{ v})} \quad \text{AmO}_2\text{(OH)}_2$$

(−0.9 v)

These are *formal potentials* and are defined as the measured potentials
corrected to unit concentration of the substances entering into the reactions.
The hydrogen-hydrogen-ion couple is taken as zero volts, and no correc-
tions are made for activity coefficients—that is, idealized conditions are
assumed. The measured potentials were established by cell, equilibrium,
and heat of reaction determinations. The potentials for acid solution were
generally measured in 1 M perchloric acid, and, for alkaline solution, in
1 M sodium hydroxide. Estimated values are given in parentheses.

The increasing stability of the III oxidation state, with increasing atomic
number in the actinide series, is illustrated by the increasing difficulty of
oxidation above the III oxidation state. This is clearly shown by the oxidation potentials and is illustrated in Figure 36, in which the oxidation poten-

FIGURE 36. *Aqueous formal oxidation potentials of the actinide ions
for the III–IV couple.*

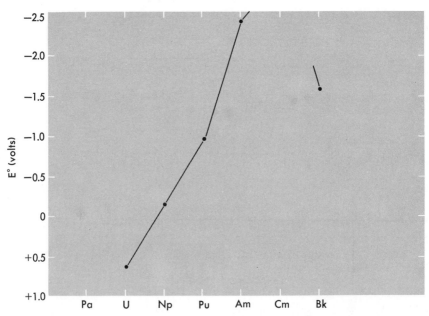

tial for the oxidation of the III to the IV state is plotted against increasing atomic number. Note the decrease in oxidation potential at berkelium, which is due to its position as the first element beyond the midpoint of the series (curium), as explained in Chapter 8.

The $M^{3+} - M^{4+}$ and $MO_2^+ - MO_2^{2+}$ reactions are readily reversible and reactions are rapid with other one-electron reducing or oxidizing agents involving no bond changes. The rate varies with reagents that normally react by two-electron or bond-breaking changes. The $M^{3+} - MO_2^+$, $M^{3+} - MO_2^{2+}$, $M^{4+} - MO_2^+$, and $M^{4+} - MO_2^{2+}$ reactions are not reversible, presumably because of slowness introduced in the making and breaking of metal-oxygen bonds.

Table 10 presents a summary of the oxidation-reduction characteristics of actinide ions. The disproportionation (i.e., self-oxidation and reduction) reactions of UO_2^+, Pu^{4+}, PuO_2^+, and AmO_2^+, are very complicated and have been studied extensively. In the case of plutonium, the situation is

Table 10   STABILITY OF ACTINIDE IONS IN AQUEOUS SOLUTION

Ion	Stability
U^{3+}	aqueous solutions evolve hydrogen on standing
Np^{3+}	stable to water, but readily oxidized by air to Np^{4+}
Pu^{3+}	stable to water and air, but easily oxidized to Pu^{4+}; oxidizes slightly under the action of its own alpha radiation (in form of Pu^{239})
Am^{3+}	stable; difficult to oxidize
Cm^{3+}	stable
Bk^{3+}	stable; can be oxidized to Bk^{4+}
Cf^{3+}	stable
Es^{3+}	stable
Fm^{3+}	stable
Md^{3+}	stable
U^{4+}	stable to water, but slowly oxidized by air to UO_2^{2+}
Np^{4+}	stable to water, but slowly oxidized by air to NpO_2^+
Pu^{4+}	stable in concentrated acid, e.g., $6M$ HNO_3, but disproportionates to Pu^{3+} and PuO_2^{2+} at lower acidities
Am^{4+}	known in solution only as complex fluoride ion; otherwise evidently disproportionates to Am^{3+} and AmO_2^+
Cm^{4+}	known in solution only as complex fluoride ion
Bk^{4+}	stable; easily reduced to Bk^{3+}
UO_2^+	disproportionates to U^{4+} and UO_2^{2+}; most stable at $10^{-4} - 10^{-2}$ M acid
NpO_2^+	stable; disproportionates only at high acidities
PuO_2^+	always tends to disproportionate to Pu^{4+} and PuO_2^{2+} (ultimate products); most stable at very low acidities
AmO_2^+	disproportionates in strong acid to Am^{3+} and AmO_2^{2+}; reduces fairly rapidly under the action of its own alpha radiation at low acidities (in form of Am^{241})
UO_2^{2+}	stable; difficult to reduce
NpO_2^{2+}	stable; easy to reduce
PuO_2^{2+}	stable; easy to reduce; reduces slowly under the action of its own alpha radiation (in form of Pu^{239})
AmO_2^{2+}	reduces fairly rapidly under the action of its own alpha radiation (in form of Am^{241})

especially complex, since four oxidation states (III, IV, V, and VI) can exist together in aqueous acidic solution in equilibrium with each other at appreciable concentrations. This is a unique situation. Although many elements have several oxidation states in solution, very few instances are known where significant concentrations of the various oxidation states occur at equilibrium. This makes the study of plutonium chemistry in aqueous solution extraordinarily complicated, but at the same time more than ordinarily rewarding.

Hydrolysis and Complex-ion Formation

Hydrolysis and complex-ion formation are closely related phenomena and therefore will be discussed together. Of the actinide ions, the small, highly-charged M^{4+} ions exhibit the greatest degree of *hydrolysis* (interaction with solvent water) and complex-ion formation. For example, the ion Pu^{4+} hydrolyzes extensively and also forms very strong anion complexes. The hydrolysis of Pu^{4+} is of especial interest in that polymers that exist as positive colloids can be produced; the molecular weight and particle size of the polymeric plutonium (IV) species depend on the method of preparation. Polymeric plutonium with a molecular weight as high as 10^{10} has been reported.

The degree of hydrolysis or complex-ion formation decreases in the order $M^{4+} > MO_2^{2+} > M^{3+} > MO_2^{+}$. The MO_2^{+} ion can almost be regarded as a large, singly-charged cation of the alkali metal type. Presumably, the relatively high tendency toward hydrolysis and complex-ion formation of MO_2^{2+} ions is related to the high concentration of charge on the metal atom (M). For the ions M^{4+} and M^{3+}, beginning at about uranium, the degree of hydrolysis increases with atomic number, but for the other two ions, MO_2^{+} and MO_2^{2+}, the degree of hydrolysis decreases with increasing atomic number.

The extensive hydrolysis of protactinium in its important V oxidation state is noteworthy because it is a trait which makes the chemical investigation of protactinium extremely difficult. Simple ions of protactinium (V) do not exist in aqueous solution and, to prevent hydrolysis, the ion must be held in solution by a complexing agent, such as a fluoride ion.

The tendency toward complex-ion formation, as for hydrolysis, of the actinide ions is determined largely by the factors of ionic size and charge. Although there is some variation within each of the ionic types, the order of complexing power of different anions with the actinides is, in general, in the order fluoride > nitrate > chloride > perchlorate for singly-charged anions, and carbonate > oxalate > sulfate for doubly-charged anions. The actinide ions form somewhat stronger complex ions than their lanthanide ion counterparts.

Actinide ions form complex ions with a large number of organic substances which render them soluble in these substances. Reaction with these substances varies from element to element and depends markedly on oxidation state. A number of important separation procedures, especially for the industrial-scale separation of plutonium, are based on this property. Organic solvents which react in this way and are immiscible in water, so that they can be used to extract plutonium from aqueous solutions, are tributyl phosphate, diethyl ether, ketones such as diisopropyl ketone or methyl isobutyl ketone, and several glycol ether-type solvents such as diethyl Cellosolve (ethyleneglycoldiethyl ether) or dibutyl Carbitol (diethyleneglycoldibutyl ether).

A number of other organic compounds—for example, acetylacetone, ethylenediaminetetraacetic acid, and cupferron—form compounds with aqueous actinide ions (in the IV state for reagents mentioned) that can be extracted from aqueous solution into immiscible organic solvents. The chelate complexes are especially noteworthy and, among these, the ones formed with diketones—such as 2-thenoyltrifluoroacetone—are of importance in separation procedures for plutonium.

Metallic State

The actinide metals, like the lanthanide metals, are highly electropositive. They can be prepared by the electrolysis of molten salts or by the reduction of a halide with an electropositive metal such as calcium or barium. Their physical properties are summarized in Table 11.

The rather technical designations for crystal structure in Table 11 are included for completeness.

Metallic protactinium, uranium, neptunium, and plutonium, have complex crystal structures that have no counterparts among the lanthanide elements. Americium is the first actinide metal to show a resemblance in crystal structure to the lanthanide metals.

Plutonium metal has very unusual metallurgical properties. It is known to exist in six allotropic modifications between room temperature and its melting point. One of the most interesting features of plutonium metal is the contraction undergone by two of its phases (delta and delta-prime) with increasing temperature. Also noteworthy is the fact that for no phase do both the coefficient of thermal expansion and the temperature coefficient of resistivity have the conventional sign (i.e., normally a metal expands on heating with an increase in electrical resistivity). The resistance decreases if the phase expands on heating. These observations on this most unusual metal pose a real challenge to the scientists concerned with the theory of the metallic state.

Solid Compounds

The tripositive actinide ions resemble the tripositive lanthanide ions in their precipitation reactions. Tetrapositive actinide ions are similar in precipitation behavior to Ce^{4+}. Thus, the fluorides and oxalates are insoluble in acid solution, and the nitrates, sulfates, perchlorates, and sulfides, are all soluble in water. The tetrapositive actinide ions form water-insoluble

Table 11 PROPERTIES OF ACTINIDE METALS

Element	Melting Point, °C	Heat of Vaporization and Boiling Point, kcal/mole	Phase	Range of Stability, °C	Crystal Structure*	Density, g/cm³ at °C
actinium	1100 ± 50	(70)			FC cubic	
thorium	1750	130–177 (3000–4200°C)	α	RT to 1400	FC cubic	11.724, 25°
			β	1400 to 1750	BC cubic	
protactinium	(<1873)	106.7 (3818°C)			tetragonal	15.37
uranium	1132		α	RT to 668	orthorhombic	19.04, 25°
			β	668 to 774	tetragonal	18.11, 720°
			γ	774 to 1132	BC cubic	18.06, 805°
neptunium	637 ± 2		α	RT to 280 ± 5	orthorhombic	20.45, 25°
			β	280 ± 5 to 577 ± 5	tetragonal	19.36, 313°
			(γ	577 ± 5 to 637 ± 2	cubic)	(18.00, 600°)
plutonium	639.5	80.46 ± 0.34 (3235°C)	α	RT to 122	monoclinic	19.737, 25°
			β	122 to 203	BC monoclinic	17.77, 150°
			γ	203 to 317	orthorhombic	17.19, 210°
			δ	317 to 453	FC cubic	15.92, 320°
			δ'	453 to 477	tetragonal	15.99, 465°
			ε	477 to 639.5	BC cubic	16.48, 500°
americium	995 ± 4°C	57 (2607°C)	α	RT to ~600	hexagonal	13.67, 20°
curium	1340°C		?		hexagonal	

* FC, face centered; BC, body centered.
Estimates and uncertain quantities are in parentheses.

iodates. The MO_2^+ actinide ions can be precipitated as the potassium salt from strong carbonate solutions. In solutions containing a high concentration of sodium and acetate ions, the actinide MO_2^{2+} ions form the insoluble, crystalline $NaMO_2(CH_3COO)_3$. The hydroxides of all four ionic types are insoluble in water; in the case of the MO_2^{2+} ions, compounds of the type exemplified by sodium diuranate ($Na_2U_2O_7$) can be precipitated from alkaline solution.

A great many compounds of the actinide elements have been prepared, and the properties of some of the important ones are summarized in Table 12. (Here again technical designations for crystal structure are included for completeness.) The binary compounds—with carbon, nitrogen, silicon, and sulfur—are not included, although these are of interest in the applications of nuclear energy because of their stability at high temperatures.

A particularly interesting triad of compounds is UF_6, NpF_6, and PuF_6. These are all highly volatile solids that can be readily volatilized at room temperature. Uranium hexafluoride gas is used for the separation of uranium-235 by the application of gaseous diffusion to the natural mixture of $U^{235}F_6$ and $U^{238}F_6$. Plutonium hexafluoride is exceedingly reactive. It is so potent a fluorinating agent that it can react even with the noble gas xenon to form the ionic compound $Xe^+ PuF_6^-$. (The analogous $Xe^+ PtF_6^-$ compound has also been prepared.) The volatile actinide fluorides thus present a most unusual group of compounds and have particular value for the study of electronic configuration in the gas phase.

The standard techniques used in inorganic chemistry, modified in the direction of microchemical methods because of the small amounts of material available or the radioactivity of the material, are used to prepare actinide compounds. Table 13 indicates some of the methods employed in the synthesis of some common actinide compounds.

Crystal Structure and Ionic Radii

Crystal structure data have provided the basis for the ionic radii of the actinide elements that are summarized in Table 14. It can be noted that for both M^{3+} and M^{4+} ions there is an *actinide contraction* (i.e., decrease in ionic radius) analogous to the lanthanide contraction (for which data are also included), with increasing positive charge on the nucleus. This contraction is a consequence of the addition of successive electrons to an inner f electron shell, so that the imperfect screening of the increasing nuclear charge by the additional f electron results in a contraction of the outer or valence orbital.

As a consequence of the ionic character of most actinide compounds and of the similarity of the ionic radii for a given oxidation state, analogous compounds are, in general, structurally identical (*isostructural*). In some cases (for example, UBr_3, $NpBr_3$, $PuBr_3$, $AmBr_3$), there is a change in structural type with increasing atomic number, which is consistent with the contraction in ionic radius that takes place. The stability of the MO_2 structure (fluorite type) is especially noteworthy, as it leads to the existence of such

CHEMICAL AND PHYSICAL PROPERTIES OF THE ACTINIDE ELEMENTS

Table 12 PROPERTIES OF SOME IMPORTANT
ACTINIDE COMPOUNDS

Compound	*Color*	*Melting Point, °C*	*Crystal Structure*
ThH_2	black		tetragonal
Th_4H_{15}	black		cubic
PaH_3	black		cubic
$\beta\text{-}UH_3$	black		cubic
Np_4H_{15}	black		
PuH_2	black		cubic
PuH_3	black		hexagonal
AmH_2	black		cubic
Am_4H_{15}	black		cubic
Ac_2O_3	white		hexagonal
Pu_2O_3			hexagonal
Am_2O_3	tan		hexagonal
	reddish-brown		cubic
Cm_2O_3	white		cubic
ThO_2	white	~3050	cubic
PaO_2	black		cubic
UO_2	brown to black	2800 ± 200	cubic
NpO_2	apple-green		cubic
PuO_2	yellow-green to brown	~1750	cubic
AmO_2	black		cubic
CmO_2	black		cubic
AcF_3	white		hexagonal
UF_3	black	>1140 (dec)	hexagonal
NpF_3	purple or black		hexagonal
PuF_3	purple	1425	hexagonal
AmF_3	pink		hexagonal
CmF_3			hexagonal
$AcCl_3$	white		hexagonal
UCl_3	red	835	hexagonal
$NpCl_3$	white	~800	hexagonal
$PuCl_3$	emerald-green	760	hexagonal
$AmCl_3$	pink		hexagonal
$AcBr_3$	white		hexagonal
$CmCl_3$	light yellow		hexagonal
$CfCl_3$			hexagonal
UBr_3	red	730	hexagonal
$\alpha\text{-}NpBr_3$	green		hexagonal
$\beta\text{-}NpBr_3$	green		orthorhombic
$PuBr_3$	green	681	orthorhombic
$AmBr_3$	white		orthorhombic
ThF_4	white	1111	monoclinic
PaF_4	reddish-brown		monoclinic
UF_4	green	960	monoclinic
NpF_4	green		monoclinic
PuF_4	brown	1037	monoclinic
AmF_4	tan		monoclinic
CmF_4			monoclinic
$ThCl_4$	white	770	tetragonal
$PaCl_4$	greenish-yellow		tetragonal
UCl_4	green	590	tetragonal
$NpCl_4$	red-brown	538	tetragonal
UF_6	white	64.02/1137 mm	orthorhombic
NpF_6	brown	53	orthorhombic
PuF_6	reddish-brown	50.75	orthorhombic

Table 13   SYNTHETIC METHODS FOR PREPARATION OF
SOME ACTINIDE COMPOUNDS

Compound	Preparative Method	Comments
Hydrides	H_2 on metals	decomposition of hydride by heating produces finely divided metal which is useful starting point for the preparation of many other compounds
Oxides	O_2 on metals or decomposition of an oxygen-containing compound, such as a hydroxide, nitrate, or oxalate	for elements with multiple oxidation states, many phases with variable composition can occur
Fluorides	for the lower fluorides, HF on oxides; for higher fluorides, additional use of F_2 or O_2	
Chlorides	HCl on oxide; Cl_2 on metal or hydride; chlorination of oxides with CCl_4, $COCl_2$, S_2Cl_2, $BrCl_3$, or other powerful chlorinating agents (a lower form, such as UCl_3, may require the use of H_2 as a reducing agent)	
Bromides	Br_2 on metal or hydrobromination of oxides	
Iodides	I_2 on metal or HI on metal	

Table 14   IONIC RADII OF ACTINIDE AND
LANTHANIDE ELEMENTS

No. of 4f or 5f electrons	Lanthanide Series				Actinide Series			
	Element	Radius A	Element	Radius A	Element	Radius A	Element	Radius A
0	La^{3+}	1.061			Ac^{3+}	1.11	Th^{4+}	0.99
1	Ce^{3+}	1.034	Ce^{4+}	0.92	(Th^{3+})	(1.08)	Pa^{4+}	0.96
2	Pr^{3+}	1.013	Pr^{4+}	0.90	(Pa^{3+})	(1.05)	U^{4+}	0.93
3	Nd^{3+}	0.995			U^{3+}	1.03	Np^{4+}	0.92
4	Pm^{3+}	(0.979)			Np^{3+}	1.01	Pu^{4+}	0.90
5	Sm^{3+}	0.964			Pu^{3+}	1.00	Am^{4+}	0.89
6	Eu^{3+}	0.950			Am^{3+}	0.99		
7	Gd^{3+}	0.938			Cm^{3+}	0.98		
8	Tb^{3+}	0.923	Tb^{4+}	0.84				
9	Dy^{3+}	0.908						
10	Ho^{3+}	0.894						
11	Er^{3+}	0.881						
12	Tm^{3+}	0.869						
13	Yb^{3+}	0.858						
14	Lu^{3+}	0.848						

Predicted values are in parentheses.

solid compounds as PaO_2, AmO_2, and CmO_2, despite the instability of the IV oxidation state of these elements in solution. The actinide contraction and the isostructural nature of the compounds constitute some of the best evidence for the transitional character of this group of elements.

Absorption and Fluorescence Spectra

The absorption spectra of actinide ions, in aqueous solution and in crystals, contain narrow bands in the visible, near-ultraviolet, and near-infrared, regions of the spectrum. There is much evidence to indicate that these bands arise from electronic transitions between energy states within the 5f electron subshell. In general, the absorption bands of the actinide ions are about ten times more intense than those of the lanthanide ions, where similar absorption spectra are observed due to electronic transitions between energy states within the 4f electron subshell.

Fluorescence is generally observed in actinide compounds under the proper conditions for excitation. It is observed, for example, in. the trichlorides of uranium, neptunium, plutonium, americium, and curium, diluted with lanthanum chloride, through the action of ultraviolet radiation.

10

Nuclear Properties

of the Actinide

Elements

Preceding chapters have dealt with methods of preparing transuranium elements, their chemical properties, and certain applications of their nuclear properties. Throughout these discussions, it could be inferred that the radioactive properties were immensely important in identifying the many isotopes and in determining how they could be prepared. The radioactive properties also determine which species can be accumulated in sufficient quantities for work with macroscopic amounts, for nuclear fuel, or for other uses. It remains now to show that the radioactive properties follow certain interesting regularities and that the study of them yields important information on the structure of nuclei in general.

The years since the discovery of the first transuranium element have seen the discovery of approximately one hundred radioactive isotopes in the transuranium region (see Appendix for detailed listing of radioactive properties and nuclear reactions for formation of known isotopes of the transuranium elements). The term *radioactivity* implies that we are dealing with unstable nuclei, and among the lighter elements such nuclei are specifically unstable with respect to radioactive decay through the emission of beta particles (negative or positive electrons). *Beta radioactivity* results from one form of nuclear instability common to all regions of the periodic system, but among the heavy elements, nuclei may decay by *alpha particle* emission and *spontaneous fission* as well. Since these forms of instability are independent of each other, a particular nuclear species may be observed to decay by any one or all three modes, depending upon the relative rates. Further, the specific characteristic of the decay of transuranium isotopes generally changes in a uniform manner from element to element, so that the decay properties of isotopes of undiscovered elements, or of undiscovered isotopes of known elements, can generally be predicted successfully.

The demands upon the techniques for observing and working with radioactive nuclides depend not only on the radioactive properties, but also upon how much of the particular nuclide can be made. This point was emphasized in Chapter 2, where it was explained that in the discovery of mendelevium only about one atom could be made per experiment! Beyond the identification as such of a radioactive nuclide (for which relatively few atoms are often sufficient), there is a strong incentive for making larger numbers of atoms so that important details of the radioactivity may be examined. It is through these details that much can be learned about nuclear structure.

Nuclear Reactions—Methods of Production

The two general methods of making nuclides, by means of neutron-capture reactions and charged-particle reactions, were discussed in earlier chapters. Many species of interest can be made only by employing accelerated protons, helium ions, or heavier ions. It is a general rule that the probability that a nucleus will capture a charged particle such as one of these is expressed by the *geometrical cross section*. (The unit of nuclear length for the designation of nuclear radii or diameters is 10^{-13} cm, and is known as a *fermi;* and the unit of nuclear cross section is 10^{-24} cm^2, and is known as a *barn.*) What this means is that a heavy nucleus appears to the incoming particle as an opaque geometrical body with a radius of about 10^{-12} centimeters (ten fermis) corresponding to a geometrical cross section, πr^2, of about 3×10^{-24} cm^2 (three barns). The captured particle brings much energy into the nucleus, and this energy must be dissipated by expelling (boiling out) particles or by other means. One of these processes —for example, the boiling out of three neutrons—may result in just the product which is sought. It is plain to see that if among all of the modes by which the energy may be dissipated the one of interest is rare, only a small fraction of the geometrical cross section will be used productively, and the cross section for the particular reaction of interest may be very small —such as millibarns (10^{-3} barn) or microbarns (10^{-6} barn) or less.

In the heavy element region, particularly as one goes to higher and higher atomic numbers, more and more of the totally available cross section goes into the fission reaction. If we bombard thorium with helium ions, some 10 per cent of the geometrical cross section may be distributed among the formation of uranium, protactinium, and thorium isotopes; the remainder ends up in fission. If, however, we bombard curium with carbon or nitrogen ions, the yield of (i.e., the cross section for the production of) an element 102 isotope will correspond to only about one-millionth of the total cross section (i.e., the sum of the cross sections for all reactions); hence, this cross section is on the order of a microbarn. It is in large part for these reasons that we know relatively little at present about detailed nuclear properties of the heaviest nuclei.

The concept of cross section (probability of reaction) for the capture of a thermal or slow neutron by a nucleus is more complicated, leading to values for such cross sections that are, in general, greater than the geometrical cross sections. *Thermal neutrons* are very low energy neutrons that have been slowed down by collisions with light nuclei such as hydrogen to the point where they have average kinetic energy about the same as that which they would have if they existed as a monatomic gas at room temperature. This corresponds to an average energy of about 0.025 electron volts, or an average velocity of about 2200 meters per second. The potentially large capture cross section is due to the wave nature of the neutron. The neutron's wave length extends its potential interaction over a very much larger area than that defined by considering it as a particle (geometrical cross section). (Cross sections greater than one million barns have been observed, e.g., xenon-135 has a 3,150,000 barn cross section for thermal neutrons.)

Thus, for example, the "Big Three" fissionable nuclides—plutonium-239, uranium-235, and uranium-233—have cross sections of 738, 582, and 588 barns (i.e., units of 10^{-24} cm^2) for fission with thermal neutrons. These three nuclides undergo fission with thermal (slow) neutrons because each contains an odd number of neutrons. The addition of a neutron to an odd-neutron nuclide involves the pairing of neutrons, which means that more *binding energy* (mass excess of neutron which is converted into energy) is available as excitation energy than is the case for the compound nuclei formed from neutron capture by neighboring isotopic even-neutron nuclei. Thus with such odd-neutron nuclides, the capture of a thermal neutron provides sufficient excitation energy to overcome the potential barrier (see explanation in following sections on alpha decay and spontaneous fission) so that fission occurs, whereas nuclides like uranium-238 and thorium-232 require fast (energy of the order of one Mev) neutrons in order to induce the fission reaction.

Alpha Decay

Decay by the emission of alpha particles (helium nuclei) is theoretically possible when the mass of a nucleus (A) is heavier than the sum of the masses of the helium nucleus (He) and the decay product, designated as A-4:

mass of A > mass of decay product (A-4) + mass of helium

In considering energies of nuclear reactions, *masses* are often used as the equivalent of an energy scale on the basis of the relationship $E = mc^2$. Atomic masses, rather than nuclear masses, can be and usually are used in considerations of the type illustrated here.

The technique of mass spectroscopy has provided rather accurate data on atomic masses, and it is possible to deduce from these that almost all species beyond the middle of the periodic system meet this requirement for alpha-instability. The general trend is that the heavier the element, the more favorable are the energetics for emission of alpha particles. This is important because the rate of alpha decay is strongly energy-dependent, and many unstable nuclei are "stable" for all practical purposes since their decay rates are negligible.

Most nuclides for which alpha radioactivity can be demonstrated experimentally are in the region above lead and bismuth. However, there have been a number of nuclides, mostly synthetic in origin, discovered mainly in the rare-earth region, that also decay by the emission of alpha particles. The explanation for the apparent end to the alpha-decay process (with the noted, and other, exceptions) in the region below lead is the very stable nuclear structure associated with the nuclide lead-208, which has a *closed shell* of protons ($Z = 82$) and neutrons ($N = 126$). (These closed nuclear shells are analogous to the closed electron shells to be found in the rare gases in the Periodic Table.)

All of the nuclei among the actinide elements should be measurably unstable toward alpha particle decay, but in some cases beta-particle emissions or spontaneous fission are so much more rapid that, effectively, the alpha-decay mode is not observed.

The measured lifetimes for alpha-particle decay have a good theoretical explanation. Even though an alpha particle within a heavy nucleus is energetically unstable with respect to its emission from the nucleus, the positive charge of the nucleus creates a zone of potential energy about it much greater than the kinetic energy of the alpha particle. In ordinary (Newtonian) mechanics, the alpha particle would have to remain within the nucleus forever, unless some external force could be applied to elevate it above the potential barrier. In *quantum mechanics,* however, there is a finite probability that the alpha particle will penetrate or leak or tunnel through the barrier. It is the rate of this *potential barrier penetration* which is so highly dependent upon the decay energy and in large part accounts for the huge variation in half-lives. This penetration rate makes it virtually impossible to observe alpha decay in the heavy element region if the alpha-particle energy is less than 4 Mev, yet causes the half-life to be extremely short if the energy is only twice as great—that is, 8 Mev. It is an important fact that alpha-particle decay energies follow predictable trends; therefore, it is possible to know fairly well what half-lives to expect for unknown nuclei.

There are only three nuclides above bismuth sufficiently long-lived to have survived geological time—thorium-232, uranium-235, and uranium-238. These nuclides are responsible for the fact that there still exist on earth small amounts of the elements between those with the atomic numbers 83 and 92, for these intermediate elements arise as products of the decay of uranium and thorium. Thus, the existence of this small "island" of relative stability at thorium and uranium is the only factor preventing the termination of the Periodic Table at bismuth, at least insofar as elements found in nature are concerned.

As these three long-lived nuclei decay, they maintain their various daughter products in equilibrium with them in amounts that depend on their relative stability or half-lives. For example, radium-226 is one of the decay products of uranium-238. Since the respective half-lives of these isotopes are 1600 years and 4.5 billion years, the two are found together in the ratio of one part of radium to three million parts of uranium, or a third of a gram of radium to a ton of uranium. One can picture the crude analogy of a large reservoir of water (uranium) trickling at a constant rate into a barrel with a hole in its bottom. The amount of water in the barrel (radium) at equilibrium will depend upon the rate at which water enters (decay rate of uranium) and the size of the hole (decay rate of radium). Two of the elements with extremely short half-lives—elements 85 and 87—are almost missed completely in the radioactive-decay series; element 87 occurs in uranium only in the fantastically low concentration of a few parts per billion billion. In the case of element 85, the amount that has been detected in nature is much smaller. Such elements cannot be isolated feasibly in macroscopic quantities and are measurable only through their radioactivity.

It is only by the grace of an odd combination of unusual circumstances, by the way, that fissionable uranium-235 still exists in the earth in sufficient quantity to provide us with nuclear chain reactors and nuclear energy. Uranium-235 has a half-life of only 0.7 billion years, which means that more than 90 per cent has disappeared through radioactive decay during the billions of years of the earth's age. Thus, only by the slenderest of margins does enough uranium-235 remain in natural uranium to operate a nuclear reactor (e.g., for the production of plutonium-239) or to make its separation from uranium-238 feasible.

Recent studies of alpha radioactivity have shown that uranium-235 falls into a category of nuclei whose half-lives are longer than would be predicted simply from their decay energy—the principal factor influencing the half-life. Even among this group, in which alpha decay is said to be *hindered,* uranium-235 is usual. For its particular decay energy, it might be expected to decay about ten times more rapidly than it does; even if its decay were only twice as rapid as it actually is, it would have essentially disappeared from the earth by this time.

Above uranium, alpha decay half-lives again become progressively shorter, so the transuranium elements of primordial origin are no longer present, although there is every reason to believe that such elements were formed at the same time as the more stable ones. Up to uranium and somewhat beyond, spontaneous fission is not an "important" mode of decay. This mode does begin to compete favorably with alpha decay around element 98, and it is possible that the ultimate limit in the preparation of transuranium elements will be set by spontaneous fission decay.

The understanding of the regularities of the alpha-decay process has been extremely useful in studying the actinide elements. It has been possible to predict alpha-particle decay energies and half-lives of as yet undiscovered isotopes and to design the experiments to observe the isotopes with a minimum of trial and error. Figures 37 and 38 illustrate the regularities of the alpha decay process, as seen in the transuranium elements. The extreme dependence of half-life upon decay energy is clearly evident in Figure 37 (note the logarithmic scale), as is the change in decay energy with the mass of a given transuranium element in Figure 38. The minima in the curves of Figure 38 occur for nuclides with about 152 neutrons, representing a sort of nuclear "subshell" configuration of special stability, which might not continue for the heavier elements. Estimated alpha particle energies for undiscovered nuclides from Figure 38 can, by referring to Figure 37, be used to predict half-lives.

The regular dependence of half-life on the energy of the alpha particle (Figure 37) pertains to nuclei with even numbers of both protons and neutrons (so-called *even-even nuclei*). Nuclei with an even number of protons and an odd number of neutrons (*even-odd nuclei*), or odd number of protons and either even or odd number of neutrons (*odd-even* or *odd-odd nuclei*) decay at slower rates than those corresponding to the curves in Figure 37 or, in the case of odd atomic numbers, than those

FIGURE 37. *Plot of the logarithm of the half-life of even-even isotopes versus the alpha-decay energy. Predictions are shown by dotted lines. Half-lives of nuclides with odd nucleons are longer than those shown or predicted here.*

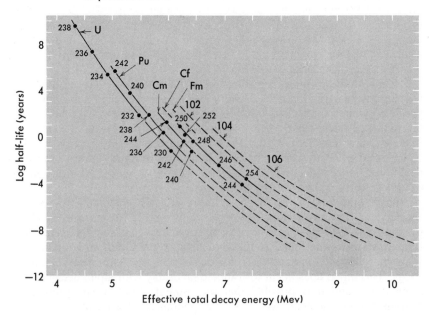

FIGURE 38. *Alpha-decay energies for the isotopes of the transuranium elements as a function of mass number. Meaning of symbols: ○ experimental value; □ calculated from a decay cycle; ● estimated value; △ calculated from a cycle containing estimated energies; ? total decay energy in question. Predictions are shown by dotted lines.*

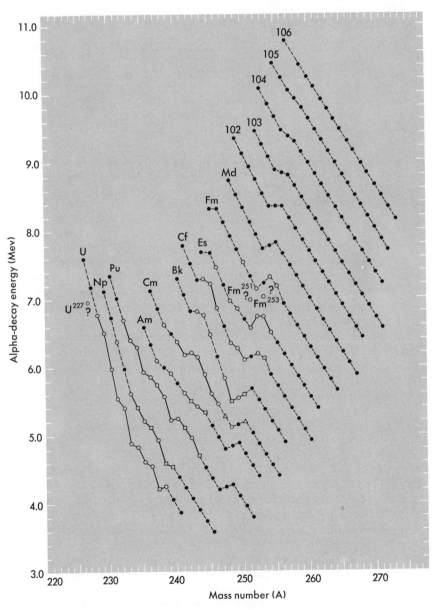

corresponding to intermediate curves interpolated in Figure 37. Such *hindered* decay therefore corresponds to longer half-lives for such nuclei.

Beta Decay

Whereas alpha-particle decay is to be found almost solely in the heavy element region and all nuclides above bismuth are alpha unstable, beta-particle decay is not unique in this region of the Periodic Table and not all heavy nuclides are beta unstable. For example, the plutonium isotopes of mass numbers 236, 238, 239, 240, 242, and 244, are all *beta stable*. If these isotopes were not unstable toward the independent process of decay by the emission of alpha particles with half-lives of less than some 100,000,000 years, they would be found in nature. (The summary of radioactive properties in the Appendix designates which of the transuranium nuclides are beta stable.) The stable isotopes of thallium, lead, and bismuth —the heaviest "nonradioactive" elements found in nature—are beta stable, in common with the stable isotopes throughout the Periodic Table.

Beta decay arises from a specific nuclear process in which a nuclear proton is converted to a neutron, or vice versa, thereby changing the atomic number of the nucleus by one unit, and making it either smaller or larger with no change in mass number (i.e., one isobar is converted to a neighboring isobar). Nuclei which have a *neutron excess* emit an electon (β^- decay); those which are *neutron deficient* absorb an orbital electron (electron capture decay) and are designated by the term "E.C." in the summary table of radioactive properties in the Appendix. An alternative process for neutron deficient nuclei which accomplishes the same end is the emission of a positron (β^+ decay), but this process is not prominent in the heavy element region.

The regularities of beta-decay energies and lifetimes in the heavy element region are not as obvious as in the case of alpha decay, and it would seem difficult to make predictions for isotopes not yet observed. However, considerable work has gone into the establishment of the *nuclear thermodynamics* of this region of the Periodic Table, utilizing the known and predicted alpha-decay energies, the known beta-decay energies, and the known atomic masses of the various nuclides. It has been possible to construct *closed decay energy cycles*. Such cycles are extremely useful in checking the internal consistency of the decay data and in predicting decay properties. Figure 39 illustrates a few such closed cycles for the so-called *4n + 1 nuclear type*. (Since alpha decay changes the mass number by four units and beta decay does not change the mass number, four nuclear types result that can be interrelated in this manner by radioactive decay; these are designated as the *4n, 4n + 1, 4n + 2,* or *4n + 3 types,* depending upon whether the mass numbers in a given type are divisible by 4 with a remainder of 0, 1, 2, or 3.)

Conservation of energy demands that the summation of decay energies around the complete cycle be exactly zero. In those cases where experimental data or reliable estimates are available for three branches of the cycle, the fourth can then be calculated by difference. Such closed decay cycles can be constructed throughout the transuranium region for each of the four nuclear types ($4n$, $4n + 1$, $4n + 2$, and $4n + 3$), thus making it possible to predict many beta-decay values and to construct complete tables of atomic masses of the transuranium nuclides. This method for predicting beta-decay values is especially useful in conjunction with alpha-

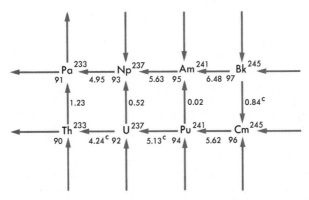

FIGURE 39. *Decay cycles for part of the $4n+1$ nuclear type. Arrows $\leftarrow$ mean alpha decay, $\uparrow$ beta decay, $\downarrow$ electron capture decay. Numbers indicate total-decay energies in Mev; those with superscript c are calculated by closing the cycles; those unmarked represent measured values.*

decay values which can be predicted through the use of figures like Figure 37. (Complete decay cycles and tables of atomic masses for each of the $4n$, $4n + 1$, $4n + 2$, and $4n + 3$, nuclear types in the heavy element region can be found in *The Transuranium Elements,* listed in the Suggested Further Readings.)

Spontaneous Fission

Nuclear fission represents an alternative means of nuclear decay for the heaviest nuclides, primarily because of the large energy release involved. It can be estimated that the energy released (i.e., decrease in mass) by the *spontaneous fission* of a heavy nuclide, e.g.,

$$_{98}Cf^{252} \longrightarrow \, _{56}Ba^{142} + \, _{42}Mo^{106} + 4\,_{0}n^{1}$$

is about 200 Mev. The distinction between this reaction and the neutron-induced fission of plutonium or uranium (discussed earlier in this chapter and in Chapter 6) is that of radioactive decay, as compared to a process brought about by a nuclear reaction. The latter type (*induced fission*) requires the additional energy, including binding energy, provided by the capture of the neutron to initiate the fission reaction; in the former case, no external influence is necessary to stimulate the fission reaction.

The first experimental observation of decay by this process was in uranium-238 by G.N. Flerov and K.A. Petrzhak in the U.S.S.R. in 1940. As with alpha decay, the half-life of this mode of decay is strongly dependent on the charge and mass of the nucleus. Spontaneous fission, together with alpha decay, becomes the limiting factor in the production of heavier and heavier transuranium elements. Decay by spontaneous fission is designated by the term "S.F." in the summary table of radioactive properties in the Appendix.

The regularities observed for spontaneous fission in the very heavy elements are shown in Figure 40.

Again, this uniformity makes it feasible to predict decay properties of undiscovered nuclides (but it is necessary to use methods that are somewhat more sophisticated than that illustrated by Figure 40). It can be noted that the lifetimes for decay by spontaneous fission begin to become comparable to those of decay by alpha-particle emission by the time element 100 is reached.

It is of some interest to examine why (in Figure 40) the half-life is related to the expression Z^2/A, where Z is the atomic number and A is the mass number or isotopic weight. One theory of fission treats the nucleus as a liquid drop which, in principle, can go through various oscillations, one mode of which would be to elongate and separate into two drops. The ease of elongation then becomes a criterion for the rate at which it will undergo spontaneous fission. More specifically, since the process involves

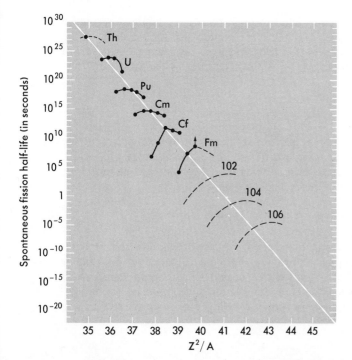

FIGURE 40. *Plot of the logarithm of spontaneous fission half-life versus Z^2/A for even-even nuclides. Half-lives for nuclides with odd nucleons are longer than shown or predicted here.*

potential barrier penetration similar to that in alpha decay, the "ease of elongation" will determine the *logarithm* of the half-life.

The instability of such a liquid drop may be described mathematically. The charge carried by the protons in the nucleus will tend to deform the drop because of the force of repulsion between like charges (Coulomb force). The Coulomb energy of a uniformly charged drop of radius, R, is proportional to the square of the charge divided by the radius. Since the charge is given by the atomic number Z, we have for the Coulomb energy, E_c:

$$E_c = k_1 \frac{Z^2}{R}$$

where k_1 is a proportionality constant whose value we do not need to know for the present purpose.

The force which tends to keep the drop from deforming is simply due to the attractive force between neutrons and protons, and the associated energy can be related to the surface tension. The surface energy, E_s, is then proportional to the surface of the drop, which in turn, is related to the square of the radius

$$E_s = k_2 R^2$$

where, again, k_2 is a proportionality constant.

If these two energies are equated, the condition is established for which the nucleus is just teetering on the brink of deformation. Thus:

$$k_1 = \frac{Z^2}{R} k_2 R^2$$

The "ease of deformation" is then expressed by the ratio E_c/E_s, or the following form:

$$\frac{Z^2}{R^3} = X$$

where the size of X will determine the logarithm of the half-life. The last step is to note that R^3 is proportional to the volume of the drop, as is the mass A; and therefore the magnitude of Z^2/A will determine the fission rate.

In another method of looking at the dynamics of the fission process, the role of the potential barrier can be described in somewhat more detail. The decay rate is controlled by a potential barrier (uphill climb) that must be surmounted either by adding some *activation energy* for induced fission, or by quantum mechanical tunneling, as described in the above section on alpha decay, for spontaneous fission. There is inherent instability in heavy nuclei due to the accumulation of large numbers of mutually-repelling protons in the nucleus. These repulsive forces must be balanced by attractive "nuclear forces"; furthermore, when the nucleons (protons and neutrons) in the nucleus are close together, the attractive forces must be stronger than the repulsive forces, or else the nucleus would not exist. As the nucleons are separated, e.g., start to divide into two fission fragments, the attractive forces die out fast (i.e., they have short range) and the repulsive forces become dominant; consequently, the process is now moving "downhill" toward the separation of two fission fragments. However, initially some means (activation or tunneling) must be found to cause the process to move "uphill" in order to overcome the attractive forces. The necessity to do this constitutes the barrier to fission. The repulsive energy of the protons on the nucleus is proportional to the factor $Z^2/A^{\frac{1}{3}}$; whereas, the energy associated with the attractive forces is proportional to $A^{\frac{2}{3}}$. A high spontaneous fission rate (a short lifetime) is then expected when the barrier is low, i.e., when the ratio of the repulsive energy to that associated with the attractive forces is large; thus, we find again that the spontaneous fission half-life should decrease as the ratio

$$\frac{Z^2/A^{\frac{1}{3}}}{A^{\frac{2}{3}}} = Z^2/A$$

is increased.

Obviously, these are crude treatments, and it is not surprising that the points in Figure 40 do not fall exactly on the straight line but cluster about it. The deviations might be expected to be largest in the heaviest elements, where the difference between large attractive forces and large repulsive forces is small. In this region, the behavior of the individual nucleons has a large effect on spontaneous fission half-lives. All of the points in Figure 40 pertain to nuclei which have even numbers of both neutrons and protons (even-even nuclides). It is beyond the scope of this account to explain the many differences between such nuclei and those with odd numbers of neutrons or protons or both. For the present purposes, it will just be pointed out that the spontaneous fission half-lives are much longer for even-odd, odd-even, and odd-odd nuclides (i.e., these types of nuclides undergo *retarded* spontaneous fission decay), than for even-even nuclides. This effect is obviously not covered by the simple treatments just given. As in the case of alpha decay, there is a special effect in the region of 152 neutrons (a nuclear "subshell" of particular stability), which might not continue for the heavier, undiscovered elements.

Nuclear Spectra

Detailed examination of radioactive decay also gives information on nuclear structure. This is an immense subject and only one example will be given for purposes of illustration.

Each neutron and proton in a nucleus has some definite motion described in terms of a set of nuclear *quantum numbers* which designate such features as the orbital path and the angular momentum. The totality of these individual particle motions defines the *structure* of the nucleus. The experimental approaches to the study of this structure take many forms, and one general way is to observe the results of disruption of some aspect of the structure. A change of structure is accomplished automatically by radioactive decay. Detailed analysis of the radiations results in what are termed *nuclear spectra,* and these often can give exact information on the kinds of changes which have taken place. Piece by piece, it is possible to reconstruct an amazingly complete picture of what is occurring in the minute domain of the nucleus.

In addition to individual particle motions, it is now clear that the nucleus as a whole can undergo *collective* modes of motion such as vibrations and rotations. An extreme form resulting in spontaneous fission has already been discussed. The means by which rotational motion of a nucleus is deduced by analyzing alpha-particle spectra is particularly simple to explain and will be used for illustration.

If a sample of an alpha-emitter such as plutonium-240 is placed in such a way that the alpha particles travel between the pole pieces of a large magnet, the paths of the alpha particles are curved and the curvature can be related to the energy of the alpha particles. A photographic plate as a detector for the emerging alpha particles completes a *spectrograph,* analogous in some ways to the use of a prism and photographic plate for analyzing light rays. In this experiment, it should be noted that there are several groups of alpha particles displaced in energy from each other by accurately measurable amounts.

The first stage in the interpretation is to note that when a large number of plutonium-240 nuclei undergo disintegration, a certain number will give off alpha particles of one discrete energy, others will give rise to another alpha group, and so on. In this case, the highest energy group is also the most intense and corresponds to a transition in which plutonium-240 decays to the uranium-236 nucleus in its lowest possible energy state (*ground state*). The other groups represent transitions to states of uranium-236 in which there is some extra energy (*excited states*). This information is summarized in the form of the decay scheme of Figure 41. Here, the excited states of uranium-236 are shown according to the excitation energies deduced from the alpha spectrum.

The numbers shown as *nuclear spin* numbers refer to the angular momentum of each of these configurations and are not directly obtained from the alpha spectrum. These come from interpretation of the gamma-ray pattern, based on the knowledge that all even-even nuclei have "zero spin" in their ground states. The excited states of uranium-236 undergo transition to the ground state through loss of energy by the emission of *gamma rays* (electromagnetic radiation) or extranuclear electrons (termed *converted* gamma rays). We theorize that this group of states can be explained as configurations in which the designated angular momenta are carried as rotational waves going around the nuclear surface. If this is the correct interpretation, the theory states that the energies of successive states should go as

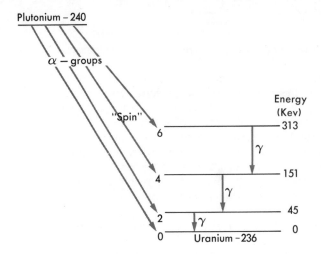

FIGURE 41. *Plutonium-240 alpha spectrum. The excited states of uranium-236 lose energy by transition to lower excited states through the emission of gamma-rays.*

$I (I + 1)$, where I is the spin number. Note that the ratio of the spin 4 energy to the spin 2 energy should be $4 (4 + 1)/2 (2 + 1)$, or $3\frac{1}{3}$; this is very close to the ratio 151/45. Similarly, the spin 6 state should be seven times as high as the spin 2 state. It is this evidence used in conjunction with other independent evidence that provides confidence that the interpretation is correct.

Similar data about energy states can also be obtained in connection with beta decay.

The situation with respect to the energy states for even-odd, odd-even, and odd-odd nuclides, is more complicated.

Diagrams like that shown for uranium-236 are available for all nuclides for which relevant alpha or beta decay and gamma-ray data are known. Such cases are indicated by multiple entries of alpha (α) and beta (β) decay energies in the table of radioactive properties in the Appendix.

The lifetimes (or half-lives) of nuclear excited states are usually so short as to make measurement very difficult or impossible. However, some such nuclear energy levels decay with measurable half-lives, or even long half-lives, when their nuclear spin numbers are considerably different from those of the ground states. Such an energy state is referred to as an *isomer* of the ground state; and its decay to the ground state, through the emission of highly converted gamma rays, is referred to as an *Isomeric Transition*. Such nuclides are designated with the superscript "m," and such decays are designated by the term "I.T." in the table of radioactive properties in the Appendix.

Postscript

This brings to a conclusion this rather brief summary of what is known about the transuranium elements. The limited scope of the treatment has, of course, made it necessary to omit much interesting information that is now available. Also, some of the information is too complicated and of too advanced a nature for inclusion here.

It is hoped that the student with a special interest in this increasingly important field will go on to read some of the available material. A list of suggested references is given below.

SUGGESTED FURTHER READING

Glasstone, Samuel, *Sourcebook on Atomic Energy,* 2nd ed. Princeton: D. Van Nostrand Co., Inc., 1958.

Jacobowitz, Henry, *Fundamentals of Nuclear Energy and Power Reactors.* New York: John F. Rider Publisher, Inc., 1959.

Katz, J. J. and G.T. Seaborg, *The Chemistry of the Actinide Elements.* New York: John Wiley & Sons, Inc., 1957. Comprehensive review of the chemistry of the actinide elements with extensive references.

Proceedings of the First United Nations International Conference on the Peaceful Uses of Atomic Energy, Geneva, 1955, United Nations, New York, 1955. *Proceedings of the Second United Nations International Conference on the Peaceful Uses of Atomic Energy,* Geneva, 1958, United Nations, Geneva, 1958. Current information relating to all phases of nuclear energy.

Seaborg, G.T., and J. J. Katz, eds., *The Actinide Elements,* National Nuclear Energy Series, Div. IV, 14A. New York: McGraw-Hill Book Co., 1949. Comprehensive description of chemical and nuclear properties of the actinide elements.

———— and E.G. Valens, *Elements of the Universe.* New York: E.P. Dutton Co., Inc., 1958. Survey of chemical elements for the high school student.

————, *The Transuranium Elements.* New Haven: Yale University Press, 1958. Survey of the chemical and nuclear properties and the history of the transuranium elements.

————, J. J. Katz, and W.M. Manning, eds., *The Transuranium Elements: Research Papers,* National Nuclear Energy Series, Div. IV, 14B. New York: McGraw-Hill Book Co., 1949.

Strominger, D., J.M. Hollander, and G.T. Seaborg, *Table of Isotopes,* Reviews of Modern Physics 30 (2), Part II, 585 (1958). Complete listing of known isotopes and their radioactive decay characteristics.

U.S. Department of Defense, *The Effects of Nuclear Weapons,* rev. ed. Washington: U.S. Atomic Energy Commission, April 1962. Superintendent of Documents, U.S. Government Printing Office, Washington 25, D.C., $3.00.

APPENDIX

Radioactive Decay Properties of Transuranium Nuclides

a Energy of radiation in million electron volts.   E.C. = electron capture.
I.T. = isomeric transition.   S.F. = spontaneous fission.

ISOTOPE	HALF-LIFE	MODE OF DISINTEGRATION a	FORMATION
Neptunium			
Np^{231}	~50 m	α (6.28)	U^{238} (d, 9n)
			U^{235} (d, 6n)
Np^{232}	~13 m	E.C.	U^{233} (d, 3n)
Np^{233}	35 m	E.C. (>99%)	U^{235} (d, 4n)
		α (10^{-3}%) (5.53)	U^{233} (d, 2n)
Np^{234}	4.4 d	E.C. (>99%)	U^{235} (d, 3n)
		$\beta+$ (4.6×10^{-2}%)	U^{236} (d, 4n)
		(0.8)	U^{235} (α, p4n)
			Pa^{231} (α, n)
			U^{234} (d, 2n)
			U^{233} (d, n)
			U^{233} (α, p2n)
			U^{233} (α, 3n) $Pu^{234} \xrightarrow{\text{E.C.}}$
			U^{235} (p, 2n)
Np^{235}	410 d	E.C. (>99%)	U^{235} (d, 2n)
		α (1.6×10^{-3}%)	U^{235} (α, p3n)
		(5.095, 5.015, 4.925,	
		4.864)	U^{235} (α, 4n) $Pu^{235} \xrightarrow{\text{E.C.}}$
			U^{233} (α, pn)
			U^{233} (α, 2n) $Pu^{235} \xrightarrow{\text{E.C.}}$
Np^{236}	>5000 y		U^{238} (d, 4n)
Np^{236m}	22 h	$\beta-$ (57%) (0.52, 0.36,	Np^{237} (n, 2n)
		0.48)	U^{238} (d, 4n)
		E.C. (43%)	U^{235} (d, n)
			U^{235} (α, p2n)
			Np^{237} (α, αn)
			U^{233} (α, p)
Np^{237m_2}	5.4×10^{-9} s	I.T. (0.27)	U^{237} $\beta-$ decay
Np^{237m_1}	6.3×10^{-8} s	I.T. (0.060)	Am^{241} α decay
			U^{237} $\beta-$ decay
Np^{237}	2.20×10^6 y	α (4.781, 4.764 plus	U^{237} $\beta-$ decay
		others ranging from	
		4.87 to 4.52)	
		β stable	
Np^{238}	2.10 d	$\beta-$ (1.25, 0.28, 0.25)	U^{238} (d, 2n)
			Np^{237} (n, γ)
			U^{238} (α, p3n)
			U^{235} (α, p)

ISOTOPE	HALF-LIFE	MODE OF DISINTEGRATION [a]	FORMATION
Np^{239}	2.35 d	$\beta-$ (0.64, 0.43, 0.33, 0.21)	U^{239} $\beta-$ decay U^{238} (d, n) U^{238} (α, p2n)
Np^{240}	7.3 m	$\beta-$ (2.16, 1.59, 1.26, 0.76)	U^{240} $\beta-$ decay Np^{239} (n, γ)
Np^{240m}	60 m	$\beta-$ (0.9)	U^{238} (α, pn) Np^{239} (n, γ)
Np^{241}	16 m	$\beta-$ (1.36)	U^{238} (α, p)
Plutonium			
Pu^{232}	36 m	E.C. ($\sim$90%) α ($\sim$10%)(6.58)	U^{235} (α, 7n) U^{233} (α, 5n)
Pu^{233}	20 m	E.C. ($>$99%) α (0.1%)(6.30)	U^{233} (α, 4n)
Pu^{234}	9.0 h	E.C. (94%) α (6%)(6.196, 6.145, 6.025)	U^{235} (α, 5n) U^{233} (α, 3n) Cm^{238} α decay
Pu^{235}	26 m	E.C. ($>$99%) α (3×10^{-3}%)(5.85)	U^{235} (α, 4n) U^{233} (α, 2n)
Pu^{236}	2.85 y	α (5.763, 5.716, 5.610, 5.448) β stable	U^{235} (d, n) Cm^{240} α decay U^{235} (α, 3n) U^{238} (α, 6n) Np^{237} (d, 3n) Np^{237} (α, p4n) Np^{237} (α, 5n) $\xrightarrow{\text{E.C.}}$ U^{233} (α, n) Np^{236} $\beta-$ decay Cm^{241} α recoils
Pu^{237m}	0.18 s	I.T. (0.145)	
Pu^{237}	45.6 d	E.C. ($>$99%) α (3.3×10^{-3}%)(5.65, 5.36)	U^{238} (α, 5n) U^{235} (α, 2n) Np^{237} (d, 2n)
Pu^{238}	86.4 y	α (5.491, 5.452, 5.352) β stable	U^{238} (d, 2n) Cm^{242} α decay Np^{237} (n, γ) $Np^{238} \xrightarrow{\beta-}$ U^{238} (α, 4n) U^{238} (α, p3n) $Np^{238} \xrightarrow{\beta-}$ U^{235} (α, n) U^{235} (α, p)
Pu^{239m_2}	1.93×10^{-7} s	I.T. (0.392)	Cm^{243} α decay Np^{239} $\beta-$ decay
Pu^{239m_1}	1.1×10^{-9} s	I.T. (0.286)	Cm^{243} α decay Np^{239} $\beta-$ decay
Pu^{239}	24,360 y	α (5.147, 5.134 plus others ranging from 5.10 to 4.92) β stable	Np^{239} $\beta-$ decay

APPENDIX

ISOTOPE	HALF-LIFE	MODE OF DISINTEGRATION [a]	FORMATION
Pu^{240}	6580 y	α (5.159, 5.115 plus others ranging from 5.01 to 4.85) β stable	Pu^{239} (n, γ) U^{238} (α, pn) $Np^{240} \xrightarrow{\beta-}$
Pu^{241}	13.2 y	β− (>99%)(0.0205) α (5 × 10^{-3}%)(4.890, 4.845)	Pu^{240} (n, γ) U^{238} (α, n) Cm^{245} α decay
Pu^{242}	3.79 × 10^5 y	α (4.898, 4.854) β stable	Pu^{241} (n, γ) Am^{242m} E.C. decay
Pu^{243}	4.98 h	β− (0.58, 0.49)	Pu^{242} (n, γ)
Pu^{244}	7.6 × 10^7 y	α (4.55 est.) β stable	Pu^{243} (n, γ) U^{238} multiple neutron capture
Pu^{245}	10.6 h	β−	Pu^{244} (n, γ)
Pu^{246}	10.85 d	β− (0.33, 0.15)	Pu^{245} (n, γ)
Americium			
Am^{237}	1.3 h	E.C. (99%) α (5 × 10^{-3}%)(6.01)	Pu^{239} (d, 4n)
Am^{238}	1.86 h	E.C.	Pu^{239} (d, 3n) Pu^{239} (p, 2n) Np^{237} (α, 3n)
Am^{239}	12 h	E.C. (>99%) α (5.0 × 10^{-3}%)(5.78)	Pu^{239} (d, 2n) Np^{237} (α, 2n) Pu^{239} (p, n) Pu^{239} (α, p3n)
Am^{240}	51 h	E.C.	Pu^{239} (d, n) Np^{237} (α, n) Pu^{239} (α, p2n)
Am^{241}	458 y	α (5.476, 5.433 plus others ranging from 5.54 to 5.24) β stable	Pu^{241} β− decay
Am^{242}	16.01 h	β− (84%)(0.667, 0.625) E.C. (16%)	Am^{241} (n, γ)
Am^{242m}	152 y	I.T. (0.049) β− (<2% of I.T.) α (0.48%)	Am^{241} (n, γ)
Am^{243}	7950 y	α (5.267, 5.224 plus others ranging from 5.340 to 5.169) β stable	Am^{242m} (n, γ) Pu^{243} β− decay
Am^{244m}	26 m	β− (>99%)(1.485)	Am^{243} (n, γ)
Am^{244}	10.1 h	β− (0.387)	Am^{243} (n, γ)
Am^{245}	1.98 h	β− (0.905)	Pu^{245} β− decay
Am^{246}	25 m	β− (2.10, 1.60, 1.35)	Pu^{246} β− decay

ISOTOPE	HALF-LIFE	MODE OF DISINTEGRATION [a]	FORMATION
Curium			
Cm^{238}	2.5 h	E.C. ($\sim$99% est.) α ($\sim$1% est.) (6.50)	Pu^{239} (α, 5n)
Cm^{239}	2.9 h	E.C.	Pu^{239} (α, 4n)
Cm^{240}	26.8 d	α (6.25, 6.21)	Pu^{239} (α, 3n)
Cm^{241}	35 d	E.C. (99%) α (1%) (5.94, 5.93, 5.88)	Pu^{239} (α, 2n)
Cm^{242}	162.5 d	α (6.110, 6.066 plus others ranging from 5.97 to 5.20) β stable	Pu^{239} (α, n) Am^{242} $\beta-$ decay
Cm^{243}	32 y	α ($>$99%) (5.780, 5.736 plus others ranging from 6.061 to 5.58) E.C. (0.3%)	Cm^{242} (n, γ)
Cm^{244}	17.6 y	α (5.801, 5.759, 5.661, 5.515) β stable	Cm^{243} (n, γ) Am^{243} (n, γ) $Am^{244m} \xrightarrow{\beta-}$ Pu^{239} multiple neutron capture
Cm^{244m}	$>10^{-5}$ s	I.T. (1.032)	Am^{244} $\beta-$ decay
Cm^{245}	9320 y	α (5.36, 5.31) β stable	Cm^{244} (n, γ) Pu^{239} multiple neutron capture U^{238} multiple neutron capture
Cm^{246}	5480 y	α (5.37) β stable	Cm^{245} (n, γ) Pu^{239} multiple neutron capture U^{238} multiple neutron capture
Cm^{247}	1.64×10^7 y	α β stable	Pu^{239} multiple neutron capture U^{238} multiple neutron capture
Cm^{248}	4.7×10^5 y	α (90%) (5.054) S.F. (10%) β stable	Pu^{239} multiple neutron capture U^{238} multiple neutron capture Cf^{252} α decay
Cm^{249}	64 m	$\beta-$ (0.86)	Cm^{248} (n, γ) Pu^{239} multiple neutron capture U^{238} multiple neutron capture

APPENDIX

ISOTOPE	HALF-LIFE	MODE OF DISINTEGRATION [a]	FORMATION
Cm^{250}	2×10^4 y	S.F. β stable (?)	Pu^{239} multiple neutron capture U^{238} multiple neutron capture
Berkelium			
Bk^{243}	4.5 h	E.C. ($>99\%$) α (0.15%) (6.72, 6.55, 6.20)	Am^{241} (α, 2n) Am^{243} (α, 4n) Cm^{242} (d, n) Cm^{244} (d, 3n)
Bk^{244}	4.4 h	E.C. ($>99\%$) α ($6 \times 10^{-3}\%$) (6.67)	Am^{241} (α, n) Am^{243} (α, 3n)
Bk^{245}	4.98 d	E.C. ($>99\%$) α (0.1%) (6.37, 6.17, 5.89)	Am^{243} (α, 2n) Cm^{242} (α, p) Cm^{244} (d, n)
Bk^{246}	1.8 d	E.C.	Am^{243} (α, n) Cm^{244} (α, pn)
Bk^{247}	7×10^3 y	α (5.67, 5.51, 5.30)	Cf^{247} E.C. decay Cm^{244} (α, p) Cm^{245} (α, pn) Cm^{246} (α, p2n)
Bk^{248}	16 h	β^- (70%) (0.65) E.C. (30%)	Bk^{247} (n, γ) Cm^{245} (α, p) Cm^{246} (α, pn)
Bk^{249}	314 d	β^- ($>99\%$) (0.125) α ($10^{-3}\%$) (5.417, 5.03)	Pu^{239} multiple neutron capture U^{238} multiple neutron capture
Bk^{250m}	3.9×10^{-8} s	I.T.	Es^{254} α decay
Bk^{250}	193 m	β^- (1.760, 0.725)	Bk^{249} (n, γ) Es^{254} α decay
Californium			
Cf^{244}	25 m	α ($>99\%$) (7.17) E.C. (?)	Cm^{242} (α, 2n) Cm^{244} (α, 4n) U^{238} (C^{12}, 6n)
Cf^{245}	44 m	E.C. (70%) α (30%) (7.11)	Cm^{242} (α, n) Cm^{244} (α, 3n) U^{238} (C^{12}, 5n)
Cf^{246}	35.7 h	α (6.753, 6.711) β stable	Cm^{244} (α, 2n) Cm^{243} (α, n) U^{238} (C^{12}, 4n)
Cf^{247}	2.4 h	E.C.	Cm^{244} (α, n) U^{238} (N^{14}, p4n)
Cf^{248}	350 d	α (6.26) β stable	U^{238} (N^{14}, p3n) Cm^{245} (α, n) Cm^{246} (α, 2n) Cm^{247} (α, 3n) Cm^{248} (α, 4n)

ISOTOPE	HALF-LIFE	MODE OF DISINTEGRATION [a]	FORMATION
Cf^{249}	360 y	α (5.806 plus others ranging from 6.194 to 5.687) β stable	Bk^{249} $\beta-$ decay
Cf^{250}	10.9 y	α (6.024, 5.980) S.F. (0.1%) β stable	Pu^{239} multiple neutron capture Bk^{250} $\beta-$ decay Cm^{247} (α, n) Cm^{248} (α, 2n) Es^{254} α decay
Cf^{251}	800 y (est.)	α (5.844, 5.667) β stable	Pu^{239} multiple neutron capture U^{238} multiple neutron capture
Cf^{252}	2.2 y	α (97%)(6.112, 6.069, 5.970) S.F. (3%) β stable	Pu^{239} multiple neutron capture U^{238} multiple neutron capture
Cf^{253}	18 d	$\beta-$ (0.27)	Pu^{239} multiple neutron capture U^{238} multiple neutron capture
Cf^{254}	61 d	S.F. β stable	E^{254} E.C. decay Pu^{239} multiple neutron capture U^{238} multiple neutron capture
Einsteinium			
Es^{245}	1.2 m	α (7.7)	Np^{237} (C^{12}, 4n) Pu^{240} (B, xn)
Es^{246}	7.3 m	E.C. α (7.35)	U^{238} (N^{14}, 6n)
Es^{248}	25 m	E.C. (>99%) α (0.3%)(6.87)	Cf^{249} (d, 3n)
Es^{249}	2 h	E.C. (>99%) α (0.1%)(6.76)	Bk^{249} (α, 4n) Cf^{249} (α, p3n) Cf^{249} (d, 2n)
Es^{250}	8 h	E.C.	Bk^{249} (α, 3n) Cf^{249} (α, p2n) Cf^{249} (α, 3n) Fm^{250} $\xrightarrow{\text{E.C.}}$ Cf^{249} (α, H^3) Cf^{249} (d, n)
Es^{251}	1.5 d	E.C. (99.5%) α ($\sim$0.5%)(6.48)	Bk^{249} (α, 2n)
Es^{252}	$\sim$140 d	α (6.64)	Bk^{249} (α, n)

ISOTOPE	HALF-LIFE	MODE OF DISINTEGRATION [a]	FORMATION
Es^{253}	20.0 d	α (6.633, 6.592 plus others ranging from 6.62 to 6.16) β stable	Cf^{253} $\beta-$ decay Pu^{239} multiple neutron capture U^{238} multiple neutron capture
Es^{254m}	38.5 h	$\beta-$ (99.9%)(1.04, 0.381) E.C. ($\sim$0.1%)	Es^{253} (n, γ) Pu^{239} multiple neutron capture
Es^{254}	250 d	α (6.43)	Es^{253} (n, γ) Pu^{239} multiple neutron capture
Es^{255}	40 d	$\beta-$	Pu^{239} multiple neutron capture U^{238} multiple neutron capture Es^{253} (n, γ) Es^{254} (n, γ)
Es^{256}	<1 h	$\beta-$	Es^{255} (n, γ)
Fermium			
Fm^{248}	0.6 m	α (7.8)	Pu^{240} (C^{12}, 4n)
Fm^{249}	150 s	α (7.9)	U^{238} (O^{16}, 5n)
Fm^{250}	$\sim$0.5 h	α (7.43)	$Cf^{249,250,251,252}$ (α, xn) Cm^{244} (C^{12}, α 2n) U^{238} (O^{16}, 4n)
Fm^{251}	7 h	E.C. (99%) α ($\sim$1%)(6.89)	Cf^{249} (α, 2n)
Fm^{252}	23 h	α (7.05) β stable	$Cf^{249,250,251,252}$ (α, xn) Cf^{250} (Be^{9}, α 3n)
Fm^{253}	4.5 d	E.C. (90%) α (10%)(6.94)	Cf^{252} (α, 3n)
Fm^{254}	3.24 h	α (7.20, 7.16, 7.06) S.F. (0.06%) β stable	Pu^{239} multiple neutron capture Es^{254m} $\beta-$ decay
Fm^{255}	22 h	α (7.12, 7.09, 7.03, 6.97, 6.90) S.F. (2.5×10^{-5}%) β stable	Pu^{239} multiple neutron capture U^{238} multiple neutron capture
Fm^{256}	160 m	S.F. β stable	Es^{255} (n, γ) $Es^{256} \xrightarrow{\beta-}$ Es^{253} (α, n) $Md^{256} \xrightarrow{E.C.}$ Es^{253} (α, p)
$Fm > 256$	$\sim$10 d	S.F.	Pu^{239} multiple neutron capture

ISOTOPE	HALF-LIFE	MODE OF DISINTEGRATION [a]	FORMATION
Mendelevium			
Md^{255}	$\sim$30 m	E.C.	Es^{253} (α, 2n)
		α (7.34)	
Md^{256}	1.5 h	E.C.	Es^{253} (α, n)
Element 102			
102^{253} (?)	5–20 s	α (8.8)	Pu^{241} (O^{16}, 4n)
102^{254}	3 s	α (8.3)	Cm^{246} (C^{12}, 4n)
102^{255} (?)	15 s	α (8.2)	Cf^{252} (B^{10}, p6n)
102^{256}	8s	α	U^{238} (Ne^{22}, 4n)
Lawrencium			
Lw^{257}	8 s	α (8.6)	$Cf^{250, 251, 252}$ (B^{11}, xn)
			$Cf^{250, 251, 252}$ (B^{10}, xn)

Index

Abelson, P. H., 7, 35, 39
Absorption spectra, 94
Accelerator, 78; and production of new elements, 2, 3, 56
Actinide contraction, *defined*, 91
Actinide elements (*see also specific element*): complex-ion formation, 88–89; compounds, synthetic methods of preparation, 91, 93; *defined*, *v*; ionic radii, 91, 93; ionic types and colors, 84–85, 92; lanthanide elements, similarity to, 40, 46, 80, 83–84, 89; metallic states, 89, 90; nuclear properties, 95–108, 110–118 (*see also* Radioactive decay *and* Nuclear structure *and* Nuclear spectra *and* Cross section); occurrence in nature, 68–69; oxidation, 84–88; Periodic table, position in, 40; production, 71–78; properties, chemical and physical, 83–94; source, 68–78; structure, electronic, 41, 79–82, 91, 94
Actinium: compounds, 92; configuration, electronic, 81; ionic radius, 93; ionic types and colors, 84; occurrence in nature, 68; oxidation potentials and states, 84–85; production of, 71; properties, chemical and physical, 84, 85, 90, 92, 93
Activation energy, for induced fission, 105
Alpha decay (*see* Radioactive decay)
Americium: compounds, 92; discovery of, 15–18, 35, 39, 40; electronic configuration, 81; ion stability, 87; ionic radius, 93; ionic types and colors, 84; isolation, 17–18, 35; oxidation states, 84, 85, 86; Periodic table of 1944, position in, 39–40; production, 19, 73; properties, chemical and physical, 84–87, 90, 92–94; properties, metallic, 90; properties, nuclear, 101, 112
Argonne national laboratory (*see also* Metallurgical laboratory), and apparent discovery of element 102, 31; and discovery of einsteinium and fermium, 23–24
Atom, nomenclature of nucleus, 1–2

Atomic energy commission, United States, transplutonium production program, 56, 75–76
Atomic energy institute, of U.S.S.R. Academy of sciences, Moscow, 31
Atomic energy research establishment, Harwell, England, 31
Atomic mass: and considering energies of nuclear reactions, 97–98; *defined*, 2
Atomic number, *defined*, 1–2; of transuranium elements, 4
Atomic weight, *defined*, 2

Barn, *defined*, 96
Benedetti-pichler, A. A., 12
Berkelium: configuration, electronic, predicted, 81; discovery, 18–23, 35; ion stability, 87; isolation, 21, 22–23, 35; oxidation potentials and states, 82, 85, 87; properties, chemical, 82–87; properties, nuclear, 19, 46, 101, 114; separations processes, 19–20
Beta decay (*see* Radioactive decay)
Binding energy, *defined*, 97
Bismuth phosphate process, 14, 23
Browne, C. I., 26, 35

Californium: compounds, 92; configuration, electronic, predicted, 81; discovery, 18–23, 35; isolation, 21, 22, 35; oxidation states, 84; production, 74–75; properties, chemical, 84, 87, 92; properties, nuclear, 19, 46, 74, 100–101, 114–115; separations processes, 19–20
Californium-252: applications, 66–67; problems in handling, 46, 74, 75
Californium-254: applications, 66–67; occurrence in supernovae, 69; problems in handling, 74
Carrier materials, in tracer chemistry, 43
Cation-exchange resins (*see* Ion exchange adsorption-elution experiments)
Chain reaction, nuclear, *described*, 58–59, 60; utilization of energy, 58–59, 60–66
Choppin, G. R., 30, 35

Commission on atomic weights (of International union of pure and applied chemistry), 26, 30–31, 102
Complex-ion formation: of actinide and lanthanide elements, 88–89
Critical mass (*see also* Nuclear explosions), 60, 61
Cross sections, 11, 96–97
Crystal structure, of actinide elements, 89, 90, 91–92
Cunningham, B. B., 12, 18, 21, 26, 35
Curie, M., 17
Curie, P., 17
Curium: compounds, 92; configuration electronic, 81; discovery, 15–18, 35, 39, 40; ion stability, 87; ionic radius, 93; ionic types and colors, 84; isolation, 18, 35; oxidation states, 84; properties, chemical and physical, 16, 84, 87, 90–94; properties, nuclear, 100–101, 113–114; Periodic table of 1944, position in, 39–40; production, 16, 73–75; separations processes, 16
Curium-242, applications, 66–67
Curium-244, applications, 66–67

Decay (*see* Radioactive decay)
Deuterium, use in thermonuclear explosions, 62
Diamond, H., 26, 35
Dowex-1 and Dowex-50 ion-exchange resins (*see* Ion-exchange adsorption-elution experiments)

Einstein, A., 26
Einsteinium: applications, potential for production of future elements, 57; configuration, electronic, predicted, 81; discovery, 23, 24, 26, 35, 77; isolation, 26, 35; oxidation states, 84; predictions, 36; production in high flux Materials testing reactor, 26; production in thermonuclear explosion, 26, 77; properties, chemical, 84, 87; properties, nuclear, 46, 101, 115–116; separations techniques, 23–25
Electromagnetic radiation, 107 (*see also* Gamma rays)
Electron capture, 2, 102 (*see also* Radioactive decay by Beta-particle emission)

Electronic structure, 38, 41, 52, 79–82 (see also Actinide and Lanthanide elements)
Element 102: configuration, electronic, predicted, 81; discovery, 31–33; naming, 31, 33; oxidation state, predictions for, 55, 82; properties, chemical, predictions for, 55; properties, nuclear, 33, 100–101, 117; separations processes, 31–33, 78; University of California experiments, 31, 33; U.S.S.R. experiments, results, 31, 33
Eluants and elution data (see Ion-exchange adsorption-elution experiments)
Energy cycles, closed decay, 102–103
Excited states, nuclear, 108
Explosions, thermonuclear (see Nuclear explosions)

Fermi, defined, 96
Fermi, E., 6, 26, 39
Fermium: configuration, electronic, predicted, 81; discovery, 22–26, 35; in first thermonuclear explosion, 23, 77; isolation, possibility of, 26; oxidation states, 84; properties, chemical, 84, 87; properties, nuclear, 100–101, 116–117; reactions, nuclear, 24; separations processes, 23–25
Fields, P. R., 24, 35
Fission, nuclear (see Nuclear fission)
Fission, spontaneous, 103–106 (see also Radioactive decay)
Fissionable nuclides: "Big Three," 97; in nuclear explosions, 60–63; as nuclear fuel in reactors, 63–66
Flerov, G. N., 31, 33, 104
Fluorescence spectra, 94
Fried, S. M., 24, 35

Gadolin, J., 17
Gamma rays: defined, 3, 107; interpretation of patterns, 107; protective measures necessary in working with, 43, 44
Gatti, R. C., 26, 35
Ghiorso, A., 15, 19, 24, 30, 34, 35
Ground state, defined, 107

Hahn, O., 6, 39
Half-life: defined, 3; factors influencing, 98–108; of isotopes of transuranium elements, 110–117; of future transuranium elements, 52–53
Hanford engineer works, 13–14
Harvey, B. G., 30, 35
Heavy ion linear accelerator (HILAC) (see University of California at Berkeley)
Higgins, G. H., 24, 35
High flux isotope reactor (HFIR), Oak Ridge, 75, 76
Hindrance factors, in radioactive decay, 52, 99, 102
Hirsch, A., 26, 35
Huizenga, J. R., 26, 35
Hydrolysis, in actinide and transuranium elements, 88–89
Hydrogen bomb (see Thermonuclear explosions)

Implosion, in nuclear explosions, 62

Ion-exchange adsorption-elution experiments (see also specific element, separations processes): anion-exchange resins, use in, 48; apparatus, 47; cation-exchange resins, use in, 47–49; description, 46–49; elution order of ions, 47–49
Ionic radii, of actinide and lanthanide elements, 91–94
Ionic types and colors, of actinide ions in aqueous solution, 84–85
Isobars, defined, 2
Isolation, of transuranium elements (see also specific element): defined, 7; first, in weighable amount, 35
Isomer, defined, 108
Isomeric transition, defined, 108
Isotopes, of transuranium elements, 1, 45, 60, 110–117

James, R. A., 15, 35

Kennedy, J. W., 9, 10, 35, 39
Kirk, P. L., 12

Lanthanide elements: actinide and transuranium elements, similarities to, 4, 38, 39, 40, 46, 80, 83–84, 89; complex-ion formation, 88; defined, 4, 38, 39–40; ionic radii, 91, 93; oxidation states, 83; metallic states, 89; structure, electronic, 80–82
Larsh, A. E., 34, 35
Latimer, R. M., 34, 35
Lawrence, E. O., 34
Lawrence radiation laboratory, (see University of California at Berkeley)
Lawrencium: configuration, electronic, predicted, 81; discovery, 34, 35, 36; identification, chemical, possibilities for, 36, 55; properties, chemical, predicted, 54–57; properties, nuclear, 101, 117; separations processes, 34, 53, 78
Liquid drop theory of spontaneous fission (see Radioactive decay, spontaneous fission)
Lithium, as source of tritium in nuclear explosions, 62
Los Alamos scientific laboratory, 23, 26

McMillan, E. M., 7, 9, 35, 39
Magnusson, L. B., 8, 35
Manning, W. M., 26, 35
Mass numbers: of actinide and transuranium elements, longest-lived or more available isotopes, 35, 70; defined, 2
Mass spectroscopy, 98
Mech, J. F., 26, 35
Meitner, L., 39
Mendeleev, D., 30, 37
Mendelevium: configuration, electronic, predicted, 81; decay involving spontaneous fission, 28–30; discovery, 26–31, 35; production, 31, 77–78; properties, nuclear, 101, 117; separations processes, 27–29, 78
Metallic states: actinide and transuranium elements, 89, 90, 92; lanthanide elements, 89
Metallurgical laboratory, Chicago: discovery of americium

Metallurgical laboratory (Cont.) (americium-241), 16, 18; discovery of curium (curium-242), 16; first isolation of neptunium (neptunium-237), 8; first isolation of plutonium (as plutonium-239), 12–15; "Mike" thermonuclear explosion, 23, 55, 77
Morgan, L. O., 15, 35

Neptunium: compounds, 92; configuration, electronic, 81; discovery, 7–9, 35; ion stability, 87; ionic radius, 93; ionic types and colors, 84; isolation, 8, 9, 35; occurrence in nature, 68; oxidation potentials, 85, 86; oxidation states, 8, 84; production, 71–72; properties, chemical and physical, 8, 39, 84–94; properties, nuclear, 101, 110–111; separations processes, 8, 9; uranium, similarity to, 8, 39
Neutrons, 2–3: applications, 66–67; capture, multiple, 73, 77; capture, multiple, in preparation of transfermium elements, 55; defined, 1; escape, rate of, in nuclear chain reactions, 60–61, 62; fast, 60, 97; slow, or thermal, 65, 97
Nobel, A., 31
Nobel institute for physics, Stockholm, Sweden, and apparent discovery of element 102, 31
Nobelium (see Element 102)
Nuclear chain reaction (see Chain reaction, nuclear)
Nuclear explosions: applications, 55–56, 57, 60–63, 63–67; description, 60–63
Nuclear fission (see also Radioactive decay, spontaneous fission): description, 58–65, 97; discovery, 6
Nuclear reactors: applications, 58–59, 60, 63–67, 75–76; cooling or heat-transfer fluids, use in, 65; high flux, 19; High flux isotope reactor (HFIR), and production of transplutonium nuclides, 74–75; Materials testing reactor, applications, 21, 26, 73–74; power, as nuclear fuel, 63–65
Nuclear thermodynamics: closed decay energy cycles, 102–103; of heavy elements, 102
Nucleons, defined, 2
Nuclides, defined, 1

Oak Ridge national laboratory, Tennessee, and High flux isotope reactor (HFIR), 75, 76
Oxidation-reduction cycle, principle and application, 14
Oxidation stabilities, of actinide ions and compounds, 41, 84–87; of III oxidation state, 86
Oxidation states (see also specific element): of actinide elements, 83–88; of future elements, 55; of lanthanide elements, 83

Periodic table of the elements: and electronic structure, 81–82; as key to discovery of transuranium elements, 4; position of transuranium ele-

Periodic table (*Cont.*)
  ments, 7, 37–41; after World
  War II, 41; before World War
  II, 38
Perlman, I., 18, 35
Petrzhak, K. A., 104
Phillips, L., 26, 35
Plowshare program, and peaceful applications of nuclear explosions, 63
Plutonium: applications, *v*, 58–
  67; carriers, 13–14; compounds, 92; configuration, electronic, 81; discovery, 9–15, 35;
  ion stability, 87; ionic radius,
  93; ionic types and colors, 84;
  isolation, 12, 35; oxidation
  states, 5, 10, 13–14, 84–88; occurrence in nature, 68–69;
  production, 13, 58–60, 64, 72–
  73, 74–76; properties, chemical and physical, 5, 84–94;
  properties, metallic, unusual,
  5, 89, 90; properties, nuclear,
  45, 63, 100–101, 111–112; separations processes, 12–15, 59,
  89; toxicity, 5, 45; and tracer
  technique, 10, 13, 59
Plutonium-238, applications, 66,
  73
Plutonium-239, applications, 61,
  63–65; properties, nuclear,
  97
Precipitation behavior, of actinide and lanthanide elements,
  89, 91
Production, of elements (*see also
  specific element*): of actinide
  elements, 70–78; of transuranium elements, 2, 55, 56–57,
  70, 73–74, 75–78, 110–117
Protactinium: chemical investigations, difficulty in, 88; compounds, 92; configuration electronic, 81; hydrolysis, 88;
  ionic radius, 93; ionic types
  and colors, 84; oxidation
  states, 83, 84–85; and Periodic table, 4, 38, 40; production, 71; properties, chemical
  and physical, 83–94; properties, metallic, 89, 90
Pyle, G. L., 26, 35

Quantum numbers: of electron
  shells, 79; in nuclear structure, 106–107

Radioactive decay: by alpha-particle emission (alpha decay),
  3, 10, 50, 96, 97–101, 102; by
  beta-particle emission (beta
  decay), 2–3, 50, 95–96, 102–
  103; by spontaneous fission, 3,
  50, 96, 99, 103–106
Radiochemistry (*see* Tracer
  chemistry)
Rare-earth elements (*see* Lanthanide elements)
Reactors (*see* Nuclear reactors)
Recoil technique (*see* Element
  102 *and* Lawrencium, separations processes)

Savannah river plant, 59
Seaborg, G, T., 9, 10, 15, 17, 19,
  24, 30, 35, 39
Segrè, E., 6, 10, 39
Separations processes and techniques, for transuranium elements (*see also specific
  elements*): ion-exchange techniques, 46–49; separations,
  physical, recoil technique, 32–
  34, 78; solvent extraction technique, 59, 89; submicrogram
  technique, 22, 50; tracer chemistry procedures, 4, 43–44; ultramicrochemical technique,
  12, 14, 50
Sikkeland, T., 34, 35
Smith, H. L., 26, 35
Solvent extraction technique, 59;
  organic compounds of importance in, 89
Spectra, nuclear, 106–108
Spence, R. W., 26, 35
Spin numbers, nuclear, 107–
  108
Spontaneous fission (*see* Radioactive decay)
Stabilities, oxidation (*see* Oxidation stabilities)
Stellar systems, other, existence
  of transuranium elements in,
  68–69
Strassmann, F. S., 6, 39
Street, K., Jr., 19, 35
Studier, M. H., 24, 35
Supernovae, containing califor-
  nium-254, 69

Thompson, S. G., 19, 21, 24, 30,
  35
Thorium: compounds, 92; configuration, electronic, 81;
  ionic radius, 93; ionic types
  and colors, 84; occurrence in
  nature, 68; oxidation states,
  83, 84, 85; and Periodic table, 4, 38, 40–41; properties,
  chemical and physical, 83–84,
  90–93; properties, metallic, 90
Thorium-232, 97, 98; applications, 64–65
Tracer chemistry (*see also specific elements, separations
  processes*): defined, 4; potential for study of elements
  above einsteinium, 54; techniques, 8, 43–44
Transuranium elements (*see
  also specific elements*): defined, 1; military applications,
  58–63; peaceful applications,
  60, 63–67
Transuranium elements, future,
  predictions, for, 5, 36, 41; discovery, possible change in cri-
  teria for, 53; half-lives, 52–53;
  Periodic table, position in,
  40–41, 54; production, methods, 55–57, 77, 78; properties,
  chemical, 54–55; properties,
  nuclear, 100–101; stability, 52–
  54, 95–96; structures, electronic, predicted, 82

Transuranium processing facility (TPF), 75–76

"Ultra-heavy" nuclei, predictions
  for, 53–54
Ultramicrochemistry (*see also
  specific elements, separations
  processes*): techniques, 12–15,
  22, 50
Union of soviet socialist repub-
  lics (U.S.S.R.): and experiments related to investigations of element 102, 31, 33;
  and heavy-ion accelerators,
  56; and spontaneous fission,
  104
University of California, Berkeley: and discovery of transuranium elements, 7, 9, 10, 11,
  16, 19, 23, 24, 27, 31, 33, 34,
  78; and Heavy ion linear
  accelerator (HILAC) at, 31,
  34, 56, 78; and "Old radiation
  laboratory" at, 11; and 60-
  inch cyclotron at Crocker radiation laboratory, 7, 9, 10,
  11, 16, 19, 27
Uranium: compounds, 92; concentration and separation of
  plutonium in ores, 59, 69;
  configuration, electronic, 81;
  enriched, *defined*, 63; ion stability, 87; ionic radius, 93;
  ionic types and colors, 84; occurrence in nature, 68; oxidation states, 84, 85, 86; and
  Periodic table, 4, 38, 40, 41;
  properties, chemical and physical, 84–87, 90–94; properties,
  metallic, 90; properties, nuclear, 100–101; separation of
  isotopes, 58, 59
Uranium-233: applications, 61,
  63, 64, 65; production, 60;
  properties, nuclear, 97
Uranium-235: applications, 61,
  63, 64; half-life, long, reason
  for, 99; properties, nuclear,
  97, 98–99; separations processes, 58, 91
Uranium-238: applications, 64,
  72; half-life, 99; properties,
  nuclear, 64, 97, 99; separations
  processes, 58, 64

Valence electrons: *defined*, 81;
  relation to oxidation state of
  actinide and lanthanide elements, 81

Wahl, A. C., 9, 10, 35, 39
Wallmann, J. C., 22, 26, 35
Walton, J. R., 35
Werner, L. B., 12, 18, 35
Wheeler, J. A., 53

X-ray diffraction, 50 (*see also*
  Ultramicrochemistry): in identification of berkelium compounds, 22; in identification
  of californium compounds, 22–
  23; in identification of plutonium compounds, 15